THE GREAT DEPRESSION

**GREAT
SPEECHES
IN
HISTORY**

Louise I. Gerdes, *Book Editor*

Daniel Leone, *President*

Bonnie Szumski, *Publisher*

Scott Barbour, *Managing Editor*

, Inc.

ornia

Library of Congress Cataloging-in-Publication Data

The Great Depression / Louise I. Gerdes, book editor.
p. cm. — (Great speeches in history)
Includes bibliographical references and index.
ISBN 0-7377-0872-7 (pbk. : alk. paper) —
ISBN 0-7377-0873-5 (lib. : alk. paper) —
1. Depressions—1929—United States.
I. Gerdes, Louise I. II. Series.

Cover Photo: © Bettmann/Corbis
Library of Congress, 19, 35, 96, 115, 125
National Archives, 133

© 2002 by Greenhaven Press, Inc.
10911 Technology Place
San Diego, CA 92127

Printed in the U.S.A.

Contents

Chapter 1: Facing the Economic Crisis

and provide training so that Americans can get back to work.

Chapter 3: Labor Issues

must be given equal access to proper housing, public health, and education.

Chapter 6: The Legacies of the Great Depression

Foreword

*I have a dream that one day this nation will rise up and live
out the true meaning of its creed: "We hold these truths to
be self-evident: that all men are created equal."*

*I have a dream that one day on the red hills of Georgia the
sons of former slaves and the sons of former slave owners
will be able to sit down together at the table of brotherhood.*

*I have a dream that one day even the state of Mississippi, a
state sweltering with the heat of injustice, sweltering with
the heat of oppression, will be transformed into an oasis of
freedom and justice.*

*I have a dream that my four little children will one day live
in a nation where they will not be judged by the color of
their skin but by the content of their character.*

Perhaps no speech in American history resonates as
deeply as Martin Luther King Jr.'s "I Have a Dream,"
delivered in 1963 before a rapt audience of 250,000 on
the steps of the Lincoln Memorial in Washington, D.C.
Decades later, the speech still enthralls those who read or
hear it, and stands as a philosophical guidepost for contemporary discourse on racism.

What distinguishes "I Have a Dream" from the hundreds
of other speeches given during the civil rights era are King's
eloquence, lyricism, and use of vivid metaphors to convey ab-
stract ideas. Moreover, "I Have a Dream" serves not only as a
record of history—a testimony to the racism that permeated
American society during the 1960s—but it is also a historical
event in its own right. King's speech, aired live on national television, marked the first time that the grave injustice of racism

was fully articulated to a mass audience in a way that was both logical and evocative. Julian Bond, a fellow participant in the civil rights movement and student of King's, states that

> King's dramatic 1963 "I Have a Dream" speech before the Lincoln Memorial cemented his place as first among equals in civil rights leadership; from this first televised mass meeting, an American audience saw and heard the unedited oratory of America's finest preacher, and for the first time, a mass white audience heard the undeniable justice of black demands.

Moreover, by helping people to understand the justice of the civil rights movement's demands, King's speech helped to transform the nation. In 1964, a year after the speech was delivered, President Lyndon B. Johnson signed the Civil Rights Act, which outlawed segregation in public facilities and discrimination in employment. In 1965, Congress passed the Voting Rights Act, which forbids restrictions, such as literacy tests, that were commonly used in the South to prevent blacks from voting. King's impact on the country's laws illustrates the power of speech to bring about real change.

Greenhaven Press's Great Speeches in History series offers students an opportunity to read and study some of the greatest speeches ever delivered before an audience. Each volume traces a specific historical era, event, or theme through speeches—both famous and lesser known. An introductory essay sets the stage by presenting background and context. Then a collection of speeches follows, grouped in chapters based on chronology or theme. Each selection is preceded by a brief introduction that offers historical context, biographical information about the speaker, and analysis of the speech. A comprehensive index and an annotated table of contents help readers quickly locate material of interest, and a bibliography serves as a launching point for further research. Finally, an appendix of author biographies provides detailed background on each speaker's life and work. Taken together, the volumes in the Greenhaven Great Speeches in History series offer students vibrant illustrations of history and demonstrate the potency of the spoken word. By reading speeches in their historical context, students will be transported back in time and gain a deeper understanding of the issues that confronted people of the past.

Introduction

After World War I, the United States experienced a decade of prosperity and boundless optimism, but during the 1930s, optimism turned to despair. The stock market crashed on October 29, 1929, and attempts to encourage fiscal confidence after the crash failed. Banks that had invested in the market with their depositors' money collapsed. Industrial production slowed, and unemployment began to rise. Many jobless workers lost their homes and stood in bread lines for food, but charity alone could not meet the needs of the swelling ranks of the unemployed. Already beleaguered farmers produced crops for Americans who had no money with which to buy them, and then the farmers themselves went bankrupt. As the decade progressed, the economy continued to slip deeper and deeper into a prolonged depression. The crisis was so grave it came to be known as the Great Depression.

The nation's social, economic, and political leaders debated solutions to the economic crisis, and their voices challenged traditional American attitudes and values. Since its inception, the nation has fought to balance often conflicting ideals. On the one hand, Americans value individualism—the right to pursue the American dream without interference from others or the heavy hand of government. However, to ensure all Americans have the opportunity to pursue their dreams, the government is often called on to provide equal access to opportunity for American citizens. Government intervention on behalf of the oppressed or downtrodden often provokes a backlash from those who feel such action depreciates the value of self-reliance. The depression tested the limits of these conflicting ideals. Not only did many Americans sacrifice individual freedom in the face of the economic crisis, but new populations of Americans began to seek equal access to the nation's wealth. The plight of the poor, the underprivileged, and the oppressed gained attention, and these social and cultural concerns that had once been the province of the local community became national interests. The voices of those who shaped American attitudes during the depression reflect the tensions between these conflicting values. A nation of Americans that had enjoyed an unprecedented era of personal freedom and independence came to see themselves and their government in a whole new way.

A Decade of Self-Determination

During the 1920s, high rates of productivity and economic growth in America had yielded unprecedented prosperity. The gross national product rose an average of 5 percent per year, and industrial output increased by more than 60 percent for the decade. Unemployment seldom exceeded 2 percent, and annual income rose significantly from $520 to $681. Purchasing power increased, and millions of people enjoyed improved living standards. Consumers chose from new and affordable products such as automobiles, radios, phonographs, washing machines, vacuum cleaners, telephones, and sewing machines.

Americans held steadfastly to the belief that the nation's prosperity came from individual determination, the founding principle of American society. During the "Roaring Twenties," Americans believed in the self-made man who could start at rock bottom and rise to the top. People who were not born to privilege could change their circumstances by working hard. The self-made man of the twenties could achieve his dreams with the support of a free market economy motivated by self-interest. According to this philosophy, individuals were free to seek their own occupations, to enter any business, and to act as they saw fit to improve their economic welfare. Competition regulated the economy, determining not only the prices of goods and services but also wage rates. Economists of the time believed that the economy was self-regulating; any fluctuations in production, employment, and consumption would correct themselves. Since self-interest motivated and drove the economy and competition served to regulate the economy, a policy of laissez-faire (or no government intervention) prevailed, and the government kept its hands off the economic activities of individuals and business, restricting its role to mediating economic disputes.

Unfortunately, self-interest in many cases translated into greed and abuse of economic liberty while competition failed to guarantee a free market. Certain individuals and businesses began interfering with the economic freedom of others. For example, large businesses exploited small ones, monopolies controlled markets, public utilities exploited consumers, and competing employers pushed wages down. Despite the wealth of the prosperous, most Americans were still poor. And though there was an unfailing belief that prosperity would continue, business had already begun to slow, and unemployment was increasing. Farmers had been overproducing crops at reduced value, and many farmers who had been caught up in the frenzy of purchasing farm mortgage options were hopelessly in debt. Many other Americans were also investing heavily in the stock market because stock prices had been rising for some time. Furthermore, investors could buy stocks on credit, putting up only a portion of the stock price. This was advantageous when prices went up because stocks could be sold at a profit high enough to pay off the credit debt, but if prices dropped the investor would have to come up with the full purchase price from some other source. Thus, when the stock market crashed on October 29, 1929, the dreams of many self-made men of the twenties crashed along with it. Unable to pay for their investments, most speculators lost their savings, their cars, their homes, and many other possessions.

Herbert Hoover's Progressive Individualism

Herbert Hoover had assumed the presidency shortly before the stock market crashed. Hoover was a self-made millionaire and, according to historian Louis W. Liebovich, embodied the nineteenth-century hero, "the boy who rose from humble beginnings to become a successful businessman through independence, hard work, and determination. . . . Hoover represented everything most Americans hoped for—power, success, and wealth mixed with decency and compassion, not flash and conspicuous consumption."[1]

Hoover's reaction to the stock market crash, then, was not surprising: He encouraged optimism, arguing that pessimism would discourage future investment and limit production. Although Hoover formed several conferences and commissions to study the nation's economic problems, he believed the government's role was merely to advise, and his voice during the depression reflects the attitude of those who held firmly to the belief that rugged individualism would again make America prosperous. Historian Roger Biles summarizes Hoover's philosophy: "Hoover saw only failure in the heavy hand of coercive government, believing that America's history ratified the reliance of individual effort."[2]

Some authorities claim that the government's inaction turned the immediate recession into a prolonged depression. Hoover did respond, however, with some government action: The Reconstruction Finance Corporation, for example, was the first government intervention in a peacetime economy, and the Emergency Relief and Construction Act was the first time a government assumed responsibility for relief. Nevertheless, most historians argue these measures were too little too late; although Hoover continued to sanction the creation of government agencies, their role was to remain strictly advisory. While later generations have treated Hoover more kindly, his contemporaries condemned his performance. Unfortunately, even most historians and economists looking back at the depression conclude that the problem had no solution. As Geoffrey Perrett writes, "What made the Depression so appalling a human tragedy was that it could be overcome only by an event as awesome, as terrifying, and as irresistible as the Depression itself. And that was the Second World War."[3]

The Economic Decline

By the winter of 1932–1933, industrial output had practically ground to a halt while prices and interest rates fell. In December 1933, unemployment was at 24.9 percent. In 1934 the national income was $10 billion less than in 1931, just above half the 1929 level. Instead of recovering from this downturn, as economists predicted, the economy slipped deeper into depression, and economists could not offer a way out.

Agriculture was an economic sector hit particularly hard by the depression. Farm prices plummeted in reaction to the stock market crash. Farmers had huge surpluses, but consumers could not afford to buy their crops. The drop in farm income meant that many farmers could no longer meet mortgage payments, and they watched helplessly as their homes and farms were foreclosed and auctioned off. Compounding these problems, the 1930s brought serious drought, making farming even more difficult. The dust storms that choked the Midwest fueled a steady stream of migrants to the Pacific Northwest and California.

Urban families were also struggling. At its peak in 1933, unemployment affected between 12 and 15 million American workers; during the rest of the decade, the number of unemployed hovered around 8 million. At times, 25 percent of the workforce was out of a job. Most people learned to get by with less, and many got used to hunger. Historian Susan Ware remarks:

> One persistent irony of the Depression was the vast economic dislocation: want in the midst of plenty. While crops rotted in the fields because farmers did not have enough money to harvest them, people starved in the cities. People wore threadbare clothing, while bales of cotton stood unsold in southern commercial centers. Thousands of shoe workers were laid off, while people walked the streets in cardboard shoes.[4]

Looking to the Government for Help

American life had changed dramatically; unfortunately for Herbert Hoover, the impact of these changes was realized during his presidency. When Americans began to lose their jobs, charity alone could not compensate for lost income and whole communities came apart. The rugged individualism that made America great was attacked by some as the source of America's economic woes. Overcome with despair, many Americans reluctantly discarded their deeply held belief in self-reliance and turned finally to the federal government as a last resort.

Unfortunately, these Americans looked to a government unfamiliar with the role of rescuer. No president had been asked to assume responsibility for managing the American economy. In the twenties, Americans expected the government to play only a minor role in their lives. This same government was now asked to create jobs, support farmers, protect investments, and insure the future financial security of its citizens. A government that had once focused primarily on foreign affairs was expected to protect American citizens from a domestic enemy more unfamiliar than any foreign foe it had ever faced.

While the economic depression damaged Hoover and the Republicans, Franklin Delano Roosevelt's bold efforts to combat the depression while governor of New York enhanced his reputation. In 1932, Roosevelt won the nomination as the Democratic Party candidate for president. He broke with tradition and flew to Chicago to accept the nomination in person, proclaiming a "new deal" for the American people. He then campaigned energetically, calling for government intervention in the economy to provide relief, recovery, and reform. His activist approach and personal charm helped to defeat Hoover by 7 million votes in November 1932.

Although millions of people had become familiar with Roosevelt the politician, most Americans did not think of him as handicapped. Roosevelt was, however, a polio paraplegic who used a wheelchair for mobility. He had to be pulled to a standing position and lifted in and out of cars and up and down stairs. Aware that Americans of the era would not have confidence in a "crippled president," particularly when the country itself was crippled by the Great Depression, Roosevelt disguised the extent of his disability through a series of complex strategies designed to make him appear able-bodied when he appeared in public.

The contrast between Herbert Hoover and Franklin Delano Roosevelt represents the change in American attitudes from the 1920s. Unlike Hoover, Roosevelt never personally experienced poverty. He was born in Hyde Park, New York, to wealth and social position. Despite Hoover's experience, principles, and efficiency, Americans were looking for a leader, and Hoover did not have the skills for dealing with people and the flair for politics that came naturally to Roosevelt. Americans no longer wanted an efficient bureaucrat as president. They needed a strong paternal figure to lead them out of the depression.

If America wanted a president who would give the government an active role in their lives, they got it. Arguably no other president before or since has pushed the role of the executive branch to its limits like Roosevelt, who took on his paternal role openly and with the support of the people. Roosevelt made his objectives clear in his first inaugural address on Saturday, March 4, 1933:

> It is to be hoped that the normal balance of executive and legislative authority may be wholly adequate to meet the unprecedented task before us. But it may be that an unprecedented demand and need for undeclared action may call for temporary departure from that normal balance of public procedure . . . and in the event that the national emergency is still critical, I shall not evade the clear course of duty that will then confront me. I shall ask the Congress for the one remaining instrument to meet the crisis—broad Executive power to wage a war against the emergency, as great as the power that would be given me if we were in fact invaded by a foreign foe. . . . We do not distrust the future of essential democracy. The people of the United States have not failed. In their need they have registered a mandate that they want direct, vigorous action. They have asked for discipline and direction under leadership. They have made me the present instrument of their wishes. In the spirit of the gift I take it.[5]

However, some Americans did mistrust the future of democracy, and their voices reflect the fear that Roosevelt would abuse his "broad executive power," threatening individual liberty.

A New Deal for America

Once in office, Roosevelt moved quickly to address the enormous need for what he called the three Rs: relief, recovery, and reform. During his first eight days in office, Roosevelt undertook immediate action to initiate his New Deal for the American people. To halt depositor panics, he temporarily closed the banks until examiners ruled them sound. Shortly thereafter, three of every four banks reopened. Because Roosevelt said so, people concluded the banks were safe, and they began to deposit the cash they had stashed under mattresses. Raymond Moley, one of Roosevelt's top aides, maintained that "capitalism was saved in eight days."[6]

In a special session of Congress, during what became known as "the first one hundred days," Roosevelt worked to pass recovery legislation that set up agencies such as the Agricultural Adjustment Administration (AAA) to support farm prices and the Civilian Conservation Corps (CCC) to employ young men. Other agencies helped business and labor, insured bank deposits, regulated the stock market, subsidized home and farm mortgage payments, and aided the unemployed. The National Recovery Act (NRA) encouraged business leaders to work together to create codes that would control wages and prices. These measures revived confidence in the economy. Banks reopened and direct relief saved millions from starvation. But the New Deal measures also involved government directly in the nation's social and economic life as never before and resulted in greatly increased spending and unbalanced budgets, which led to criticism of Roosevelt's programs.

The Critics of the New Deal

Those who spoke against the New Deal reflect the tension the depression placed on America's often conflicting American values. Some Republicans such as Herbert Hoover and Democrats such as former Democratic presidential candidate Al Smith opposed Roosevelt's New Deal policies, arguing that they threatened individual liberty and states' rights. Although some claimed big government resembled European fascism and stifled rather than promoted business prosperity, others argued that the federal government had no right to interfere with the right of each state to determine how its farms and businesses should be run. Roosevelt's opponents declared their fears that his administration was interfering with the balance of powers established by the nation's founders.

Some of Roosevelt's critics, however, lobbied for more rather than less government intervetion, suggesting even more radical reforms to ensure all Americans had equal access to economic security. These philosophically diverse critics blamed the depression on the greed and corruption of a minority of wealthy Americans who placed the burden of the economic crisis on the poor. Father Charles Coughlin, a Catholic activist who had once supported Roosevelt, argued that despite Roosevelt's pledge to the people to protect them from greedy financial leaders, he continued to be swayed by the "money changers." Coughlin believed in even tighter regulation of big business and finance. In a similar vein, Huey Long, the controversial and dictatorial governor of Louisiana, railed that America's multimillionaires had taken too much

Franklin Delano Roosevelt

from America's banquet for themselves and must share their wealth if every American was to have an equal opportunity to experience life, liberty, and the pursuit of happiness. Long spoke of a radical program of taxation that would limit the fortunes of the wealthy. Socialist candidate Norman Mattoon Thomas declared his concern that Roosevelt's plan focused too much on the nation's economic problems, ignoring the social and moral issues that he believed fostered the nation's economic crisis.

Most Americans supported Roosevelt's efforts, however, and another flurry of New Deal legislation followed in 1935, including the establishment of the Works Projects Administration (WPA), which put 3.5 million jobless Americans to work on roads, parks, and public buildings. Moreover, the WPA provided jobs for artists, writers, musicians, and authors as well as laborers. In the past, the arts had been supported by private funding, and many objected to government support as misuse of tax dollars; some simply did not accept singing, acting, or painting as work. Artists too were concerned, as historian Robert S. McElvaine suggests, "that as Washington began paying the pianist it would want to call the tune. Even if there were no conscious interference—and who could be sure there would not be?—the possibility that bureaucracy would stifle creativity was omnipresent."[7] On the other hand, others claimed that only government support could make art accessible to all Americans and help American artists explore and develop a truly American artistic identity.

Also enacted in 1935, the Social Security Act provided unemployment compensation and a program of old-age and survivors' benefits that continues today. On June 8, 1934, President Roosevelt had created the Committee on Economic Security (CES) to study the issue of unemployment and pension payments. Under the leadership of Secretary of Labor Frances Perkins, the first women selected to a cabinet position, Congress developed a detailed legislative proposal. Although the act did not achieve all the aspirations of those who supported it, it did provide disability coverage, medical benefits, aid to dependent children, and grants to the states to provide medical care.

Facing Domestic Foes

After an overwhelming victory in the election of 1936, Roosevelt took on the critics of the New Deal, particularly the Supreme Court, which had ruled much of his legislation unconstitutional. At this point during the depression, the tension between America's conflicting ideals—rugged individualism and government paternalism—had created a great rift between New Deal supporters and opponents. In 1937, Roosevelt proposed to add new justices to the Supreme Court who would support his legislation, but critics voiced their concern that he was "packing" the Court and undermining the separation of government powers. Congress defeated his proposal, but under the leadership of Chief Justice Charles Evans Hughes, the Court began to decide in favor of several New Deal proposals, including the National Labor Relations Act and the Social Security Act. Hughes believed that it was the role of the Court to balance the needs of government with the rights of the individual; therefore, he recognized the need for public welfare in a time of crisis.

Although Roosevelt's New Deal met with vigorous opposition and would not completely cure America's economic woes, the New Deal reforms would endure, from Social Security and low-interest home mortgages to cheap electricity and a supervised stock market. Journalist Lewis Lord writes of Roosevelt: "Long before political scientists concluded he had created the modern presidency, long before economists decided he had saved capitalism, long before historians ranked him beside Washington and Lincoln as 'great,' a man who couldn't walk put America on its feet."[8] Nevertheless, by the end of the decade, New Deal reform legislation diminished, and the ills of the depression would not fully abate until the nation mobilized for war. Only during the massive spending necessary for World War II would unemployment finally slip below 15 percent.

Seeking Opportunities for All Americans

New groups that had once been alienated from the political process gained a voice during the depression, which challenged traditional notions of equal opportunity. Members of Roosevelt's administration began to speak for children, women, and racial minorities. Policy makers believed the government played an important role in promoting social justice and encouraged New Deal legislation that reflected their interest in child welfare, housing reform, and equal rights.

The New Deal did have a better record than the previous administration in helping America's youth. The National Recovery Act of 1934 and the Fair Labor Standards Act of 1938, for example, banned exploitative child labor. More than 2 million students worked on National Youth Administration (NYA) projects between 1936 and 1943, and 12.9 percent of high school jobs were given to minorities. The

Federal Emergency Relief Administration's (FERA) college aid program of 1934 funded work-study jobs. The Civilian Conservation Corps (CCC) funded jobs for another 2.6 million needy youths, and the Social Security Administration's Aid to Dependent Children provided funds for impoverished boys and girls. New Deal money also funded a free school lunch program and the construction of new schools. Furthermore, FERA funded teacher salaries, thus preventing four thousand school closings. The New Deal set a precedent for federal programs that support youth and education and provided the model for reforms well into the 1960s.

Though the administration's record supporting the rights of women and minorities was less progressive, many in Roosevelt's administration began to speak out for equal rights. Although women were still not recognized as an important part of the workforce during the depression, the WPA did have a women's division headed by Ellen Woodward, who provided a voice for working women and spoke of the importance of training those without skills so that they might become employable. Woodward's efforts to help poor women were considerable in view of American attitudes at that time. However, not until large numbers of women went to work to replace the men who went off to fight during World War II did women begin to become recognized as part of the workforce.

Roosevelt's wife, Eleanor, became a major voice in his administration on the issue of racism and equal rights. In 1939, for example, when the Daughters of the American Revolution refused to let African American opera singer Marian Anderson perform in Constitution Hall, Eleanor Roosevelt resigned her membership and arranged to hold the concert at the nearby Lincoln Memorial, turning the event into an outdoor celebration attended by seventy-five thousand people. Another voice for the equal rights of minorities was Aubrey Williams. While director of the NYA, Williams insured that funds were set aside to help promising African American graduate students, and approximately two hundred African American students received Ph.D.s during the 1930s, compared with only forty-five between 1900 and 1930.

The Urban League, however, provided a more progressive voice for the concerns of the urban African American during the depression. Founded in 1911 by Ruth Standish Baldwin and Dr. George Edmund Haynes, the Urban League was pledged to advance opportunities for the flood of African Americans who had migrated to the urban centers of the North when the Supreme Court, in the 1896 decision *Plessy v. Ferguson,* effectively approved segregation. The league began by counseling migrants and training social workers. But in 1918 the league expanded its role, campaigning to crack barriers to black employment. The league boycotted firms that refused to hire blacks, pressured schools to expand vocational opportunities, and prodded Washington officials to include blacks in New Deal programs.

During the depression, the league also began efforts to integrate trade unions and committed to collective bargaining and organized action for both African American and white workers. When American Federation of Labor (AFL) locals refused to accept African Americans, league members reminded the AFL that an integrated union was more powerful than a segregated union. League leaders urged aggressive action, including AFL legislation that excluded from membership locals that refused to accept Negro members.

The Plight of the Tenant Farmer

Some groups had to speak out on their own behalf. Many sharecroppers, tenant farmers, and their families were effectively evicted as a result of New Deal farm programs. The Agricultural Adjustment Act (AAA) of 1933 authorized the federal government to pay cash subsidies to farmers who would reduce production, but government checks went to the plantation owners, not to the sharecroppers and tenants whose rent was paid in profits from their crops. When the government told farmers to cut back production, sharecroppers and tenant farmers were forced off the land and had no way to support themselves.

Tenant farmers in east Arkansas realized that the only way they could protect their interests was by organized protests. A small group of black and white farmers met in a schoolhouse in Arkansas and formed the Southern Tenant

Farmers Union (STFU), which became a powerful force in American labor. STFU cotton pickers held a strike in the fall of 1935, and after ten days, landlords gave in and were forced to raise wages. When, in December 1935, a landlord evicted one hundred sharecroppers, the STFU protested loudly. By April 1936 Arkansas was making national headlines; the STFU hoped for federal intervention, but not until 1938 did the government agree to send payments to sharecroppers and tenants. This provided little help, however, because landlords simply evicted their sharecroppers and tenants and continued to keep the AAA money for themselves.

The Politics of Labor

One of the most successful groups to gain a voice during the depression was labor. Prior to the depression, labor was poorly organized. The typical union was a "company union," always under the watchful eye of employers. The government took little interest in labor relations and maintained a hands-off approach to business. Hoover's philosophy of progressive individualism relied on the belief that benevolent employers led grateful workers into prosperity. When Hoover's system failed, many of the unemployed began to look at radical solutions such as communism and socialism, but most turned to the government for support.

Along with his other efforts, Roosevelt directly and indirectly improved the plight of working people. Roosevelt's first response to the industrial crisis was the National Industrial Recovery Act (NIRA) of 1933, which seemed to favor business more than labor. The act encouraged businesses to cooperate in setting codes of conduct to eliminate excessive competition. Ironically, United Mine Workers (UMW) president John L. Lewis took hold of Section 7a, which dictated that every industrywide code must allow workers the right to organize unions and bargain collectively, and told miners that the president wanted them to join a union, although this was never Roosevelt's intention. Lewis and his followers organized hundreds of thousands of miners. By the end of 1933, the American Federation of Labor (AFL) had added more than a half-million members.

The NIRA was no panacea for workers because the act provided no means of enforcement, which forced workers to take alternative action. In 1934 more than a million and a half American workers went on strike, including San Francisco longshoremen who brought the city's waterfront to a standstill. When police intervened, open fighting led to the deaths of two strikers. Two weeks later in Minneapolis, another two striking teamsters were killed.

When the Supreme Court declared the NIRA unconstitutional in 1935, however, Roosevelt remained committed to labor as he recognized the importance of labor in the reform of the nation's economic system. Roosevelt now turned to New York senator Robert F. Wagner and his proposed legislation that would create a National Labor Relations Board (NLRB). The Wagner bill prohibited unfair labor practices and empowered the NLRB to investigate and punish lawbreakers. The NLRB would oversee employee elections to unionize and make sure that employers negotiated solely with unions properly elected by workers. Although opposed by business, the National Labor Relations Act became law in the summer of 1935.

The Sit-Down Strike

Also in 1935, inspired by the fiery rhetoric of labor leader John L. Lewis, automobile workers organized the United Automobile Workers of America (UAW). Auto manufacturing giant General Motors (GM) would not recognize the UAW as a bargaining representative, and battles between workers and GM management began. At GM's Fisher body plant in Cleveland, the workers were angered because the plant manager refused to discuss reductions in the number of parts a worker would have to assemble in order to receive a set pay rate. On December 28, 1936, the UAW representative walked down the line, banging on the machines with a wrench, shouting, "Sit down! Sit down!" The workers shut off the machines and sat down. They would not leave. Two days later, hearing that GM was moving work to factories without strong unions, workers in Flint, Michigan, also began a sit-down strike. Within a week, for the time being at least, GM was out of the auto-making business.

The sit-down strike was more effective than the traditional picket line because employers could far more easily replace striking employees who walked the picket line than workers who physically stayed put in the plant. During negotiations, relations between the striking employees and management remained relatively amicable. On January 11, however, Flint's uneasy truce was shattered when plant guards barred delivery of evening meals to the one hundred men occupying the plant and a GM official turned off the heat. Both sides called in reinforcements. Union toughs from Detroit headed for Flint while the police headed for the factory. Strikers seized the gate and the police fired tear gas. When the wind shifted, the police retreated under a hail of parts and debris thrown by the strikers. A few officers fired their pistols, and several workers were wounded, one seriously.

When Michigan governor Frank Murphy ordered the National Guard into Flint to keep the peace, hostilities ceased. However, when GM went to court to seek an injunction ordering the workers out, workers seized the engine plant in Flint. Infuriated that GM's rivals were building cars and GM was not, management agreed to recognize the UAW. After forty-four days, the strike was over on March 12, 1937. The success of the UAW inspired others and the power of unions continued to grow.

The Golden Age of Radio

The events at Flint were brought to national attention thanks to a rather newly marketed invention, radio. Besides carrying news, the radio gave policy makers and their opponents a forum to debate the social, economic, and political issues facing the nation. Radio knew no geographic boundaries; listeners came from urban and rural communities, from every age, culture, and class. In 1923 an estimated four hundred thousand American households had a radio; by the midthirties over 19 million households had radio sets. Entire families would gather to listen to increasingly varied programming, and the influence of radio grew exponentially.

The radio personalized events for the listener. People did

not have to read about Roosevelt's plans to rejuvenate the economy; they heard the news from the man himself. On his eighth day in office, Roosevelt (speaking from the White House) told a national radio audience why closing the banks was necessary. He did it so well, political satirist Will Rogers remarked, that even bankers could understand it. These "fireside chats" represented a bond across the airwaves between the people and their leader. On an unprecedented scale, one person could speak to, influence, and perhaps change the lives of millions.

America's first talk-radio hosts emerged during the depression. Father Coughlin had an enormous influence on depression-era America, and at the peak of his popularity, one-third of the nation tuned in to his weekly broadcasts. Father Coughlin began his radio career broadcasting sermons to children from his parish, but his broadcasts eventually shifted to economic and political issues. Initially, Coughlin's controversial broadcasts attacked Roosevelt and the New Deal, but when he began to attack Jewish figures, the Catholic Church forced him to stop his broadcasts and return to his work as a parish priest.

America's cowboy philosopher, Will Rogers, also used the radio as a forum for his political philosophy, but unlike Father Coughlin, Rogers considered himself an entertainer, not an activist. Although he claimed that "all I know is what I read in the newspaper," many Americans respected his commonsense approach to political and economic issues and were persuaded by the folksy charm Rogers used to mock himself and the public figures of his time. He spoke simply so that everyone could understand. Because his satire was aimed at Democrat and Republican alike, he appealed to a broad audience, many of whom needed a little laughter during the depression.

The Legacy of the Depression

Few historians or economists would dispute that the depression represented a remarkable change in the way Americans saw themselves. Once-powerless employees recognized they had strength in unity, crying "Sit down! Sit down!" Once alienated from the political process, working women, chil-

dren, and racial minorities found a voice in the often controversial policy makers of Roosevelt's New Deal administration. America began to develop its own artistic identity, and
artists who had once depended on private funding found
support from a government with a new vision. With the
widespread deprivation brought on by the depression,
rugged individualism had to make way for government intervention, and the expanded influence of the government in
the lives of the American people begun during the depression
continues to be the subject of debate. Those who shape contemporary policy echo the concerns of those who shaped social, economic, and political policy during America's grave
economic crisis. Both proponents and opponents of contemporary issues often mirror the rhetoric of the 1930s when
they debate endowments for the arts, public utilities, welfare,
affirmative action, and social security. While the generations
of Americans who experienced the nation's economic crisis
firsthand are passing, the influence of the depression on
American life can be heard in the voices of those who shared
their social, economic, and political philosophy in Great
Speeches in History: *The Great Depression.*

Notes

1. Louis W. Liebovich, *Bylines in Despair: Herbert Hoover, the Great Depression, and the U.S. News Media.* Westport, CT: Praeger, 1994, p. xiii.

2. Roger Biles, *A New Deal for the American People.* DeKalb: Northern Illinois
University Press, 1991, p. 16.

3. Geoffrey Perrett, *America in the Twenties: A History.* New York: Simon &
Schuster, 1982, pp. 490–91.

4. Susan Ware, *Holding Their Own: American Women in the 1930s.* New York:
Twayne, 1982, p. xiii.

5. Franklin D. Roosevelt, first inaugural address, Saturday, March 4, 1933. Taken
from the Avalon Project at the Yale Law School: Documents in Law, History,
and Diplomacy, available at www.yale.edu/lawweb/avalon/avalon.htm.

6. Quoted in Lewis Lord, "The Rise of the Common Man," *U.S. News & World
Report,* October 25, 1993, p. 10.

7. Robert S. McElvaine, *The Great Depression: America, 1929–1941.* New
York: Times Books, 1984, p. 269.

8. Lord, "The Rise of the Common Man," p. 10.

CHAPTER
ONE

Facing the Economic Crisis

Rugged Individualism Makes America Prosperous

Herbert Hoover

Herbert Hoover was born to hardworking parents but was orphaned at age six and raised by his aunt and uncle. The circumstances of his childhood instilled in Hoover a strong sense of self-reliance, industriousness, and concern for the downtrodden. Hoover became known as a humanitarian while chairman of the Commission for Relief in Belgium during World War I. He developed his laissez faire economic philosophy while serving as secretary of commerce from 1921 to 1928 under Calvin Coolidge. When Coolidge decided not to run for a second term, Hoover became the Republican presidential nominee.

Hoover's belief in the power of individual initiative and private enterprise was reflected in his campaign. He argued that during World War I it was necessary for the government to own and operate some businesses, but that America's return to rugged individualism in business affairs after the war fostered the nation's prosperity. In contrast, European paternalism and state socialism curbed individual ingenuity, paving the way for despotism. To maintain its economic growth, the United States had to avoid too much government interference in business.

The following campaign speech, delivered in New York City on October 22, 1928, reflects Hoover's political and economic philosophy. Hoover says that the government should only act as an umpire in business affairs. When government becomes involved in business, Hoover

Herbert Hoover, campaign speech, New York City, October 22, 1928.

argues, leadership is stifled, and expansion of government bureaucracy also erodes other freedoms such as freedom of speech. To preserve political freedom, claims Hoover, America must not sacrifice economic freedom. The success of free enterprise, Hoover concludes, has resulted in the near abolition of poverty in America.

On Tuesday, October 29, 1929, approximately one year after Hoover's election to the presidency, the stock market crashed, followed by a severe depression. Although Hoover encouraged state and local governments to support private charities, asked Congress to appropriate money for public-works projects, and backed the creation of the Reconstruction Finance Corporation (RFC), Hoover's actions were insufficient to alleviate hunger and unemployment. The American people blamed Hoover's "hands-off" policies. In 1932, Americans elected Franklin D. Roosevelt as president to solve the nation's economic crisis.

During one hundred and fifty years we have built up a form of self-government and a social system which is peculiarly our own. It differs essentially from all others in the world. It is the American system. It is just as definite and positive a political and social system as has ever been developed on earth. It is founded upon a particular conception of self-government in which decentralized local responsibility is the very base. . . . It is founded upon the conception that only through ordered liberty, freedom, and equal opportunity to the individual will his initiative and enterprise spur on the march of progress. And in our insistence upon equality of opportunity has our system advanced beyond all the world.

During the War we necessarily turned to the government to solve every difficult economic problem. The government having absorbed every energy of our people for war, there was no other solution. For the preservation of the state the Federal Government became a centralized despotism which undertook unprecedented responsibilities, assumed autocratic powers, and took over the business of citizens. To a large degree we regimented our whole people temporarily into a socialistic state. However justified in time of war, if continued in peace-time it would destroy not only our American system, but with it our progress and freedom. . . .

Choosing Between Opposing Doctrines

When the War closed, the most vital of all issues both in our own country and throughout the world was whether governments should continue their wartime ownership and operation of many instrumentalities of production and distribution. We were challenged with a peace-time choice between the American system of rugged individualism and a European philosophy of diametrically opposed doctrines—doctrines of paternalism and state socialism. The acceptance of these ideas would have meant the destruction of self-government through centralization of government. It would have meant the undermining of the individual initiative and enterprise through which our people have grown to unparalleled greatness.

The Republican Party from the beginning resolutely turned its face away from these ideas and these war practices. A Republican Congress co-operated with the Democratic administration to demobilize many of our war activities. At that time the two parties were in accord upon that point. When the Republican Party came into full power, it went at once resolutely back to our fundamental conception of the state and the rights and responsibilities of the individual. Thereby it restored confidence and hope in the American people, it freed and stimulated enterprise, it restored the government to its position as an umpire instead of a player in the economic game. For these reasons, the American people have gone forward in progress while the rest of the world has halted, and some countries have even gone backwards. If anyone will study the causes of retarded recuperation in Europe, he will find much of it due to stifling of private initiative on one hand, and overloading of the government with business on the other.

There has been revived in this campaign, however, a series of proposals which, if adopted, would be a long step toward the abandonment of our American system and a surrender to the destructive operation of governmental conduct of commercial business. Because the country is faced with difficulty and doubt over certain national problems—that is, prohibition, farm relief, and electrical power—our opponents propose that we must thrust government a long way into the businesses which give rise to these problems. In effect, they abandon the tenets of their own party and turn to state socialism as a solution for the difficulties presented by all three. It is proposed that we shall change from prohibition to the state purchase and sale of liquor. If their agricultural relief program means anything, it means that the government shall directly or indirectly buy and sell and fix prices of agricultural products. And we are to go into the hydro-electric power business. In other words, we are confronted with a huge program of government in business. . . .

When Government Interferes in Business

The effect would reach to the daily life of every man and woman. It would impair the very basis of liberty and freedom not only for those left outside the fold of expanded bureaucracy but for those embraced within it. Let us first see the effect upon self-government. When the Federal Government undertakes to go into commercial business, it must at once set up the organization and administration of that business, and it immediately finds itself in a labyrinth, every alley of which leads to the destruction of self-government. . . .

The first problem of the government about to adventure in commercial business is to determine a method of administration. It must secure leadership and direction. Shall this leadership be chosen by political agencies, or shall we make it elective? The hard practical fact is that leadership in business must come through the sheer rise in ability and character. That rise can only take place in a free atmosphere of competition. Competition is closed in a bureaucracy. Political agencies are feeble channels through which to select able leaders to conduct commercial business.

Government, in order to avoid the possible incompetence, corruption, and tyranny of too great authority in individuals entrusted with commercial business, inevitably turns to boards and commissions. To make sure that there are checks and balances, each member of such boards and commissions must have equal authority. Each has his separate responsibility to the public, and at once we have the conflict of ideas and the lack of decision which would ruin any commercial business. It has contributed greatly to the demoralization of our shipping business. Moreover, these commissions must be representative of different sections and different political parties, so that at once we have an entire blight upon coordinated action within their ranks which destroys any possibility of effective administration. . . .

Thus every time the Federal Government goes into a commercial business, five hundred and thirty-one Senators and Congressmen become the actual board of directors of that business. Every time a state government goes into business, one or two hundred state senators and legislators become the actual directors of that business. Even if they were supermen and if there were no politics in the United States, no body of such numbers could competently direct commercial activities; for that requires initiative, instant decision, and action. It took Congress six years of constant discussion to even decide what the method of administration of Muscle Shoals [a construction project to build a river passage and hydro-electric dam on the Tennessee River in Alabama] should be. . . .

The Benefits of Private Enterprise

During the war the government found it necessary to operate the railways. That operation continued until after the war. In the year before being freed from government operation they were not able to meet the demands for transportation. Eight years later we find them under private enterprise transporting fifteen percent more goods and meeting every demand for service. Rates have been reduced by fifteen percent and net earnings increased from less than one percent on their valuation to about five percent. Wages of employees have improved by thirteen percent. The wages of railway employees are today one hundred and twenty-one percent above pre-war, while the wages of government employees are today only sixty-five percent above pre-war. That should be a sufficient commentary upon the efficiency of government operation. . . .

The government in commercial business does not tolerate amongst its customers the freedom of competitive reprisals to

Herbert Hoover

which private business is subject. Bureaucracy does not tolerate the spirit of independence; it spreads the spirit of submission into our daily life and penetrates the temper of our people not with the habit of powerful resistance to wrong but with the habit of timid acceptance of irresistible might.

Bureaucracy is ever desirous of spreading its influence and its power. You cannot extend the mastery of the government over the daily working life of a people without at the same time making

it the master of the people's souls and thoughts. Every expansion of government in business means that government, in order to protect itself from the political consequences of its errors and wrongs, is driven irresistibly without peace to greater and greater control of the nation's press and platform. Free speech does not live many hours after free industry and free commerce die.

It is a false liberalism that interprets itself into the government operation of commercial business. Every step of bureaucratizing of the business of our country poisons the very roots of liberalism—that is, political equality, free speech, free assembly, free press, and equality of opportunity. . . .

True liberalism is a force truly of the spirit, a force proceeding from the deep realization that economic freedom cannot be sacrificed if political freedom is to be preserved. Even if governmental conduct of business could give us more efficiency instead of less efficiency, the fundamental objection to it would remain unaltered and unabated. It would destroy political equality. It would increase rather than decrease abuse and corruption. It would stifle initiative and invention. It would undermine the development of leadership. It would cramp and cripple the mental and spiritual energies of our people. It would extinguish equality and opportunity. It would dry up the spirit of liberty and progress. For these reasons primarily it must be resisted. . . .

I feel deeply on this subject because during the War I had some practical experience with governmental operation and control. I have witnessed, not only at home but abroad, the many failures of government in business. I have seen its tyrannies, its injustices, its destructions of self-government, its undermining of the very instincts which carry our people forward to progress. I have witnessed the lack of advance, the lowered standards of living, the depressed spirits of people working under such a system. My objection is based not upon theory or upon a failure to recognize wrong or abuse, but I know the adoption of such methods would strike at the very roots of American life and would destroy the very basis of American progress. . . .

Controlling Big Business

In the last fifty years we have discovered that mass production will produce articles for us at half the cost they required previously. We have seen the resultant growth of large units of production and distribution. This is big business. Many businesses must be bigger, for our tools are bigger, our country is bigger. . . .

The American people, from bitter experience, have a rightful fear that great business units might be used to dominate our industrial life and by illegal and unethical practices destroy equality of opportunity.

Years ago the Republican administration established the principle that such evils could be corrected by regulation. It developed methods by which abuses could be prevented while the full value of industrial progress could be retained for the public. It insisted upon the principle that when great public utilities were clothed with the security of partial monopoly, whether it be railways, power plants, telephones, or what not, then there must be the fullest and most complete control of rates, services, and finances by government or local agencies. It declared that these businesses must be conducted with glass pockets.

As to our great manufacturing and distributing industries, the Republican Party insisted upon the enactment of laws that not only would maintain competition but would destroy conspiracies to destroy the smaller units, or dominate and limit the equality of opportunity amongst our people. . . .

And what have been the results of our American system? Our country has become the land of opportunity to those born without inheritance, not merely because of the wealth of its resources and industry, but because of this freedom of initiative and enterprise.

Russia has natural resources equal to ours. Her people are equally industrious, but she has not had the blessings of one hundred and fifty years of our form of government and of our social system.

By adherence to the principles of decentralized self-government, ordered liberty, equal opportunity, and freedom to the individual, our American experiment in human welfare has yielded a degree of well-being unparalleled in all the world. It has come nearer to the abolition of poverty, to the abolition of fear of want, than humanity has ever reached before. Progress of the past seven years is the proof of it. This alone furnishes the answer to our opponents, who ask us to introduce destructive elements into the system by which this has been accomplished.

Let us see what this system has done for us in our recent years of difficult and trying reconstruction and then solemnly ask ourselves if we now wish to abandon it.

The Success of the American Experiment

As a nation we came out of the War with great losses. We made no profits from it. The apparent increases in wages were at that time fictitious. We were poorer as a nation when we emerged from the War. Yet during these last eight years we have recovered from these losses and increased our national income by over one-third, even if we discount the inflation of the dollar. That there has been a wide diffusion of our gain in wealth and income is marked by a hundred proofs. I know of no better test of the improved conditions of the average family than the combined increase in assets of life and industrial insurance, building and loan associations, and savings deposits. These are the savings banks of the average man. These agencies alone have, in seven years, increased by nearly one-hundred percent, to the gigantic sum of over fifty billions of dollars, or nearly one-sixth of our whole national wealth. We have increased in home ownership, we have expanded the investments of the average man.

In addition to these evidences of larger savings, our people are steadily increasing their spending for higher standards of living. Today there are almost nine automobiles for each ten families, where seven and one-half years ago, only enough automobiles were running to average less than four for each ten families. The slogan of progress is changing from the full dinner pail to the full garage. Our people have more to eat, better things to wear, and better homes. We have even gained in elbow room, for the increase of residential floor space is over twenty-five percent with less than ten percent increase in our number of people. Wages have increased, the cost of living has decreased. The job of every man and woman has been made more secure. We have in this short period decreased the fear of poverty, the fear of unemployment, the fear of old age; and these are fears that are the greatest calamities of human kind.

All this progress means far more than greater creature comforts. It finds a thousand interpretations into a greater and fuller life. A score of new helps save the drudgery of the home. In seven years, we have added seventy percent to the electric power at the elbows of our workers and further promoted them from carriers of burdens to directors of machines. We have steadily reduced the sweat in human labor. Our hours of labor are lessened; our leisure has increased. We have expanded our parks and playgrounds. We have nearly doubled our attendance at games. We pour into outdoor recreation in every direction. The visitors at our national parks have trebled, and we have so increased the number of sportsmen fishing in our streams and lakes that the longer time between bites is becoming a political issue. In these seven and one-half years, the radio has brought music and laughter, education and political discussion to almost every fireside.

A Better Way of Life

Springing from our prosperity with its greater freedom, its vast endowment of scientific research, and the greater resources with which to care for public health, we have, according to our insurance actuaries, during this short period since the War, lengthened the average span of life by nearly eight years. We have reduced infant mortality, we have vastly decreased the days of illness and suffering in the life of every man and woman. We have improved the facilities for the care of the crippled and helpless and deranged.

From our increasing resources, we have expanded our educational system in eight years from an outlay of twelve hundred-millions to twenty-seven hundred-millions of dollars. The education of our youth has become almost our largest and certainly our most important activity. From our greater income, and thus our ability to free youth from toil, we have increased the attendance in our grade schools by fourteen percent, in our high schools by eighty percent, and in our institutions of higher learning by ninety-five percent. Today we have more youth in these institutions of higher learning twice over than all the rest of the world put together. We have made notable progress in literature, in art, and in public taste.

We have made progress in the leadership of every branch of American life. Never in our history was the leadership in our economic life more distinguished in its abilities than today, and it has grown greatly in its consciousness of public responsibility. Leadership in our professions and in moral and spiritual affairs of our country was never of a higher order. And our magnificent educational system is bringing forward a host of recruits for the succession to this leadership.

I do not need to recite more figures and more evidence. I cannot believe that the American people wish to abandon, or in any way to weaken, the principles of economic freedom and self-government which have been maintained by the Republican Party, and which have produced results so amazing and so stimulating to the spiritual as well as to the material advance of the nation.

Your city [New York] has been an outstanding beneficiary

of this great progress and of these safeguarded principles. With its suburbs it has, during the last seven and one-half years, grown by over a million and a half of people until it has become the largest metropolitan district of all the world. Here you have made abundant opportunity, not only for the youth of the land, but for the immigrant from foreign shores. This city is the commercial center of the United States. It is the commercial agent of the American people. It is a great organism of specialized skill and leadership in finance, industry, and commerce which reaches every spot in our country. Its progress and its beauty are the pride of the whole American people. It leads our nation in its benevolences to charity, to education, and to scientific research. It is the center of art, music, literature, and drama. It has come to have a more potent voice than any other city in the United States.

But when all is said and done, the very life, progress, and prosperity of this city is wholly dependent on the prosperity of the 115,000,000 people who dwell in our mountains and valleys across the three thousand miles to the Pacific Ocean. Every activity of this city is sensitive to every evil and every favorable tide that sweeps this great nation of ours. Be there a slackening of industry in any place, it affects New York far more than any other part of the country. In a time of depression, one-quarter of all the unemployed in the United States can be numbered in this city. In a time of prosperity, the citizens of the great interior of our country pour into your city for business and entertainment at the rate of one hundred and fifty thousand a day. In fact, so much is this city the reflex of the varied interests of our country, that the concern of every one of your citizens for national stability, for national prosperity, for national progress, for preservation of our American system is far greater than that of any other single part of our country.

Addressing the Remaining Problems

We still have great problems if we would achieve the full economic advancement of our country. In these past few years, some groups in our country have lagged behind others in the march of progress. I refer more particularly to those engaged in the textile, coal, and agricultural industries. We can assist in solving these problems by co-operation of our government. To the agricultural industry we shall need to advance initial capital to assist them to stabilize their industry. But this proposal implies that they shall conduct it themselves, and not by the government. It is in the interest of our cities that we shall bring agriculture and all industries into full stability and prosperity. I know you will gladly cooperate in the faith that in the common prosperity of our country lies its future.

In bringing this address to a conclusion, I should like to restate to you some of the fundamental things I have endeavored to bring out. The foundations of progress and prosperity are dependent as never before upon the wise policies of government, for government now touches at a thousand points the intricate web of economic and social life.

Under administration by the Republican Party, in the last seven and one-half years, our country as a whole has made unparalleled progress, and this has been in generous part reflected to this great city. Prosperity is no idle expression. It is a job for every worker; it is the safety and the safeguard of every business and every home. A continuation of the policies of the Republican Party is fundamentally necessary to the further advancement of this progress and to the further building up of this prosperity.

I have dwelt at some length on the principles of relationship between the government and business. I make no apologies for dealing with this subject. The first necessity of any nation is the smooth functioning of the vast business machinery for employment, feeding, clothing, housing, and providing luxuries and comforts to a people. Unless these basic elements are properly organized and function, there can be no progress in business, in education, literature, music, or art. There can be no advance in the fundamental ideals of a people. A people cannot make progress in poverty.

I have endeavored to present to you that the greatness of America has grown out of a political and social system and a method of control of economic forces distinctly its own—our American system—which has carried this great experiment in human welfare farther than ever before in all history. We are nearer today to the ideal of the abolition of poverty and fear from the lives of men and women than ever before in any land. And I again repeat that the departure from our American system by injecting principles destructive to it, which our opponents propose, will jeopardize the very liberty and freedom of our people and will destroy equality of opportunity, not alone to ourselves but to our children.

My conception of America is a land where men and women may walk in ordered freedom in the independent conduct of their occupations; where they may enjoy the advantages of wealth, not concentrated in the hands of the few, but spread through the lives of all; where they build and safeguard their homes, and give to their children the fullest advantages and opportunities of American life; where every man shall be respected in the faith that his conscience and his heart direct him to follow; where a contented and happy people, secure in their liberties, free from poverty and fear, shall have the leisure and impulse to seek a fuller life.

Some may ask where all this may lead, beyond mere material progress. It leads to a release of the energies of men and women from the dull drudgery of life to a wider vision and a higher hope. It leads to the opportunity for greater and greater service, not alone from man to man in our own land, but from our country to the whole world. It leads to an America, healthy in body, healthy in spirit, unfettered, youthful, eager—with a vision searching beyond the farthest horizons, with an open mind, sympathetic and generous. It is to these higher ideals and for these purposes that I pledge myself and the Republican Party.

A Crisis Calling for Extreme Measures

Franklin Delano Roosevelt

During the early years of the depression, President Herbert Hoover believed, as did many economists and financial leaders, that left alone, the economy would eventually right itself. Business leaders operating through the spirit of competition would restore America's prosperity. Meanwhile, individual charity would protect those who were suffering from unemployment. However, when the economy did not improve during Hoover's administration, Americans began looking for a new leader, one who would take decisive action. The people found such a leader in Franklin Delano Roosevelt, who in 1932 defeated Hoover in a landslide election.

The only child of a wealthy family, Roosevelt began his political career in New York, where he was elected to the state senate in 1910. In 1920, after serving as assistant secretary of the navy under Woodrow Wilson, Roosevelt became Wilson's vice presidential nominee. Although stricken in 1921 with polio that left him a paraplegic, Roosevelt returned to politics in 1928 and was elected governor of New York. Shortly thereafter he became president, a position he would hold for four consecutive terms. And it was as the nation's chief executive that Roosevelt would redefine the role of government in economic affairs.

Roosevelt believed that the federal government should take decisive action to improve the economy. He blamed financial leaders and big business for America's economic plight and recommended government regula-

Franklin Delano Roosevelt, "First Inaugural Address," Washington, D.C., March 4, 1933.

tion of banks and industry. Roosevelt's first inaugural address, delivered on March 4, 1933, not only reflects this new economic philosophy but is considered by many to be one of the greatest inaugural addresses of any president. It was also the first inaugural address to be recorded. At the time of his speech, the audience did not respond to Roosevelt's now famous line, "the only thing we have to fear is fear itself." The newspapers only drew attention to the phrase the following day. However, the president drew cheers from the crowd after he chastised Wall Street bankers, promising to drive "the money changers from the temple." The audience also reacted when Roosevelt threatened a Congress that might refuse to pass his legislation, asking for "broad executive power." Critics on both sides would later blast Roosevelt's New Deal administration for both keeping and failing to keep these promises. While conservative Democrats and Republicans claimed Roosevelt abused his executive powers, liberal Democrats argued that he failed to drive out the money changers.

This is a day of national consecration, and I am certain that on this day my fellow Americans expect that, on my induction into the presidency, I will address them with a candor and a decision which the present situation of our people impels.

This is preeminently the time to speak the truth—the whole truth, frankly and boldly. Nor need we shrink from honestly facing conditions in our country today. This great nation will endure as it has endured, will revive and will prosper. So, first of all, let me assert my firm belief that the only thing we have to fear is fear itself—nameless, unreasoning, unjustified terror, which paralyzes needed efforts to convert retreat into advance.

In every dark hour of our national life a leadership of frankness and vigor has met with that understanding and support of the people themselves which is essential to victory. I am convinced that you will again give that support to leadership in these critical days.

In such a spirit on my part and yours, we face our common difficulties. They concern, thank God, only material things. Values have shrunk to fantastic levels; taxes have risen; our ability to pay has fallen; government of all kinds is faced by serious curtailment of income; the means of exchange are frozen in the currents of trade; the withered leaves of industrial enterprise lie on every side; farmers find no markets for their produce; the savings of many years, in thousands of families, are gone.

More important, a host of unemployed citizens face the grim problem of existence, and an equally great number toil with little return. Only a foolish optimist can deny the dark realities of the moment.

And, yet our distress comes from no failure of substance. We are stricken by no plague of locusts. Compared with the perils which our forefathers conquered, because they believed and were not afraid, we have still much to be thankful for. Nature still offers her bounty, and human efforts have multipled it. Plenty is at our doorstep, but a generous use of it languishes in the very sight of the supply.

The Failure of Financial Leaders

Primarily, this is because the rulers of the exchange of mankind's goods have failed through their own stubbornness and their own incompetence, have admitted their failure and have abdicated. Practices of the unscrupulous money-changers stand indicted in the court of public opinion, rejected by the hearts and minds of men.

True, they have tried, but their efforts have been cast in the pattern of an outworn tradition. Faced by the failure of credit, they have proposed only the lending of more money. Stripped of the lure of profit by which to induce our people to follow their false leadership, they have resorted to exhortations, pleading tearfully for restored confidence. They know only the rules of a generation of self-seekers. They have no vision, and when there is no vision, the people perish.

Yes, the money-changers have fled from their high seats in the temple of our civilization. We may now restore that temple to the ancient truths!

The measure of the restoration lies in the extent to which we apply social values more noble than mere monetary profit. Happiness lies not in the mere possession of money; it lies in the joy of achievement, in the thrill of creative effort. The joy and moral stimulation of work no longer must be forgotten in the mad chase of evanescent profits.

These dark days will be worth all they cost us if they teach us that our true destiny is not to be ministered unto but to minister to ourselves and to our fellow men. Recognition of the falsity of material wealth as the standard of success goes hand in hand with the abandonment of the false belief that public office and high political position are to be valued only by the standards of pride of place and personal profit. There must be an end to a conduct in banking and in business which too often has given to a sacred trust the likeness of callous and selfish wrongdoing.

Small wonder that confidence languishes, for it thrives only on honesty, on honor, on the sacredness of obligations, on faithful protection, and on unselfish performance. Without them it cannot live.

Putting People to Work

Restoration calls, however, not for changes in ethics alone. This nation asks for action, and action now! Our greatest primary task is to put people to work.

This is no unsolvable problem if we face it wisely and courageously. It can be accomplished, in part, by direct recruiting by the Government itself, treating the task as we would treat the emergency of a war, but at the same time, through this employment, accomplishing greatly needed projects to stimulate and reorganize the use of our natural resources.

Hand in hand with that, we must frankly recognize the overbalance of population in our industrial centers and, by engaging on a national scale in a redistribution, endeavor to provide a better use of the land for those best fitted for the land. Yes, the task can be helped by definite efforts to raise the values of agricultural products and with this the power to purchase the output of our cities. It can be helped by preventing realistically the tragedy of the growing loss, through foreclosure, of our small homes and our farms. It can be helped by insistence that the Federal, State, and local governments act forthwith on the demand that their cost be drastically reduced. It can be helped by the unifying of relief activities, which today are often scattered, uneconomical, and unequal. It can be helped by national planning for and supervision of all forms of transportation and of communications and other utilities that have a definite public character.

There are many ways in which it can be helped, but it can never be helped merely by talking about it! We must act, we must act quickly. Finally, in our progress toward a resumption of work, we require two safeguards against a return of the evils of the old order: There must be a strict supervision of all banking and credits and investments; there must be an end to speculation with other people's money. And there must be provision for an adequate but sound currency.

There are the lines of attack. I shall presently urge upon a new Congress, in special session, detailed measures for their fulfillment, and I shall seek the immediate assistance of the 48 States!

First Things First

Through this program of action, we address ourselves to putting our own national house in order and making income balance outgo. Our international trade relations, though vastly important, are in point of time and necessity secondary to the establishment of a sound national economy! I favor, as a practical policy, the putting of first things first. I shall spare no effort to restore world trade by international economic readjustment, but the emergency at home cannot wait on that accomplishment.

The basic thought that guides these specific means of national recovery is not narrowly nationalistic. It is the insistence, as a first consideration, upon the interdependence of the various elements in all parts of the United States; a recognition of the old and permanently important manifestation of the American spirit of the pioneer. It is the way to recovery. It is the immediate way. It is the strongest assurance that the recovery will endure!

In the field of world policy, I would dedicate this Nation to the policy of the good neighbor; the neighbor who resolutely respects himself and, because he does so, respects the rights of others; the neighbor who respects his obligations and respects the sanctity of his agreements in and with a world of neighbors.

If I read the temper of our people correctly, we now realize as we have never realized before our interdependence on each other; that we can not merely take but we must give as well; that if we are to go forward, we must move as a trained and loyal army willing to sacrifice for the good of a common discipline, because without such discipline no progress is made, no leadership becomes effective. We are, I know, ready and willing to submit our lives and property to such discipline, because it makes possible a leadership which aims at a larger good. This I propose to offer, pledging that the larger purposes will bind upon us—bind upon us all—as a sacred obligation with a unity of duty hitherto evoked only in times of armed strife.

Asking for Broad Executive Power

With this pledge taken, I assume unhesitatingly the leadership of this great army of our people dedicated to a disciplined attack upon our common problems. Action in this image, and to this end, is feasible under the form of government which we have inherited from our ancestors. Our Constitution is so simple and practical that it is possible always to meet extraordinary needs by changes in emphasis and arrangement without loss of essential form. That is why our constitutional system has proved itself the most superbly enduring political mechanism the modern world has ever seen. It has met every stress of vast expansion of territory, of foreign wars, of bitter internal strife, and of world relations.

And, it is to be hoped that the normal balance of executive and legislative authority may be wholly adequate to meet the unprecedented task before us. But it may be that an unprecedented demand and need for undelayed action may call for temporary departure from that normal balance of public procedure.

I am prepared under my constitutional duty to recommend the measures that a stricken nation in the midst of a stricken world may require. These measures, or such other measures as the Congress may build out of its experience and wisdom, I shall seek, within my constitutional authority, to bring to speedy adoption.

But, in the event that the Congress shall fail to take one of these two courses, and in the event that the national emergency is still critical, I shall not evade the clear course of duty that will then confront me. I shall ask the Congress for the one remaining instrument to meet the crisis—broad executive power to wage a war against the emergency as great as the power that would be given to me if we were in fact invaded by a foreign foe!

For the trust reposed in me, I will return the courage and the devotion that befit the time. I can do no less.

We face the arduous days that lie before us in the warm courage of the national unity; with the clear consciousness of seeking old and precious moral values; with the clean satisfaction that comes from the stern performance of duty by old and young alike. We aim at the assurance of a rounded, a permanent national life. We do not distrust the future of essential democracy.

The *people* of the United States have not failed. In their need they have registered a mandate that they want direct, vigorous action. They have asked for discipline and direction under leadership. They have made me the present instrument of their wishes. In the spirit of the gift, I take it.

In this dedication of a nation, we humbly ask the blessing of God. May He protect each and every one of us! May He guide me in the days to come.

Capital and Labor Must Compromise

William Allen White

Born in Emporia, Kansas, journalist and author William Allen White epitomized small-town American life. However, his well-crafted editorial writing for the *Emporia Gazette* won White international acclaim. White's liberal Republicanism reflected tolerance, optimism, and provincialism. Known as the "Sage of Emporia," White became the spokesperson for the average American.

In the following speech given before the American Management Congress on September 20, 1937, White, who rarely accepted invitations to speak, voices his economic philosophy, arguing that both capital and labor are responsible for America's economic troubles. Rather than waste time and resources fighting inevitable reforms, says White, capitalists must accept some government regulation. In addition, labor leaders must fight for the needs of labor, rather than working primarily to increase their political power. The middle class, White maintains, will eventually have its way, and to appease the middle-class consumer's demand for fair prices and a stable industry, capital and labor must learn to compromise.

I n this discussion I am supposed to represent the public—the American consumer. He is a mythical character who never lived on land or sea, but for that matter, the capitalist is a myth and the worker's status is an economic hypothesis. It is trite to say that in America we are all more or

William Allen White, speech before the American Management Congress, Washington, D.C., September 20, 1937. Reprinted by permission of Barbara White Walker.

less owners, all workers of high or low degrees, and certainly we are all consumers. We are all the children of John Q. Public, and our interests as members of the consuming public are after all our chief end and objective as citizens of our democracy.

The Mistakes of Laborers and Capitalists

Let me begin by telling you both, laborer and capitalist, that you have got us citizen consumers in a pretty sad mess. Every time we consumers think of what one of you has done we are dead sore at each of you until we begin to think of what the other has done. Let me start on capital, the employer. Not that he is more to blame than labor. But he is more responsible. He enjoys more freedom. He could have done better. You employers have wasted twenty years since the end of the [first] World War. In those twenty years, a little intelligent self-interest, a little foresight—not much—would have solved equitably the problems that are now pressing upon us, problems that have been adjusted in haste and in the emergency of calamity. Take the eight-hour day. You knew that it was coming. Why didn't you men willingly, sensibly, grant it? But no. You had to fight it, every inch, and make the consuming public think you were greedy—when you were not. You were just dumb—dumb to give labor a sense of deep antagonism. Take the old age pension and job insurance to cover seasonal and technological unemployment. A thousand voices rose across the land, telling you of the trouble ahead. What did you do? You put cotton in your ears, and if you could hear through the cotton you began yelling "Communism!" at the academician and the liberal politician and spokesmen of the consuming public. Everyone realized 20 years ago and more that sooner or later, with the pensions of the Civil War gone which took care of the aged until the World War, we should have old age pensions as a federal problem. Yet you employers let a generation of old people, unprovided for, begin to clamor for old age pensions and begin to listen to demagogues with silly panaceas. Then, having squandered your substance, you turned your men on the street in the days of the locust, and put into the hands of the most adroit politician America has ever seen the votes of ten million men whom your slipshod social viewpoint rendered jobless. If a dozen or twenty years ago you, Mr. Capitalist, had used the social sense of the average man in the street, this problem of unemployment and old age pensions would not be handing to your arch-enemies an organized, subsidized, class-conscious proletariat which can be voted to your destruction. By your sloth you created the particular head devil who is mocking you. He is your baby. You begot him two decades ago in the days of your youth when you were going to handle your business in your own way and no man could come into your shop and tell you how to run it!

But labor has been no Solomon. The proper business of a labor union is to get higher wages, better hours and good shop conditions for the workmen. But when labor en masse plunks its vote for its own party, then the spirit of party loyalty begins to obscure labor's objectives—high wages, short hours, decent shop conditions. Thus class-conscious labor leaders become more interested in their party welfare than in the fundamental objectives of labor unions. So we shall have the class-conscious political worker trading his vote not for the immediate objective of wages, hours and shop conditions, but for power for his political labor boss. The political labor boss will ask the workers to swallow a whole ticket in order to dominate a whole government. He would turn a democracy into a contest between two class-conscious parties, a class-conscious proletariat and a class-conscious plutocracy. In that setup where is the Consumer; where indeed is the compromise between labor and capital under the supervision of a middle class? In short with only two class-conscious political parties, what becomes of democracy? The labor union militant and undefiled—yes; the vertical union and the closed shop? Yes. But a class-conscious labor party in a democracy—no! If labor insists upon maintaining its class lines of bitter intransigent hostility to all capital, the American middle class—old John Q. Public and his heirs and assigns—will not support labor.

This is a middle-class country and the middle class will have its will and way. For the middle class is the real owner

FACING THE ECONOMIC CRISIS

of American industry. The middle class is also 80 per cent worker and the consumer of 80 per cent of American industrial production in the home market. The middle class thinks and feels chiefly as The Consumer. And before the middle class demands an increase in either interest for investors or higher wages for the worker, the middle class will demand fair prices and a stable industry. That means industrial peace. No peace is lasting until it is founded upon that essential equitable compromise between the contending forces—capital and labor—known as justice.

A Plan to Share the Wealth

Huey Long

Huey Long was one of the most flamboyant figures in American political history. Long's impromptu political speeches were colorful and often irreverent. He could easily switch from crude, backwoods humor to religious homilies, appealing to any audience. Long's political ambition and his popularity among the rural voters won him the governorship of Louisiana and eventually a U.S. Senate seat. Known as the "Kingfish," Long used autocratic and often ruthless methods to maintain his power and influence, which many believed overshadowed his social reforms and welfare proposals. Many considered Long a serious threat to the Roosevelt administration when, in the spring of 1935, Long tried to unite the radical movements and form a third party. His career and ambitions, however, were cut short when Long was assassinated on September 10, 1935.

Long's economic philosophy was a simple one—America needed to redistribute its wealth. To promote his plan, Long started grass-roots organizations called Share Our Wealth clubs, whose slogan was "Every Man a King." By 1935, more than 7 million people had signed up for Long's clubs. In the following radio address, aired in 1935, Long outlines his "Share Our Wealth" program. Long argues that America's multimillionaires have more than they or their families will ever need, and to allow them to maintain their fortunes while many Americans go without is unfair. To alleviate this inequity, Long outlines a program of graduated taxation on multimillion-

Huey Long, "Sharing Our Wealth," radio address, 1935.

dollar incomes that would also limit how much a person could earn. The wealth appropriated from the rich would be redistributed to give all Americans a guaranteed income as well as a home, a car, and a radio. Long's program appealed to many because of its apparent simplicity and fairness, although opponents claimed that confiscating funds from millionaires would provide less than $1.50 for each poor family.

P resident Roosevelt was elected on November 8, 1932. People look upon an elected President as the President. This is January 1935. We are in our third year of the Roosevelt depression, with the conditions growing worse. . . .

We must now become awakened! We must know the truth and speak the truth. There is no use to wait three more years. It is not Roosevelt or ruin; it is Roosevelt's ruin.

A President's Promise

Now, my friends, it makes no difference who is President or who is senator. America is for 125 million people and the unborn to come. We ran Mr. Roosevelt for the presidency of the United States because he promised to us by word of mouth and in writing:

1. That the size of the big man's fortune would be reduced so as to give the masses at the bottom enough to wipe out all poverty; and

2. That the hours of labor would be so reduced that all would share in the work to be done and in consuming the abundance mankind produced.

Hundreds of words were used by Mr. Roosevelt to make these promises to the people, but they were made over and over again. He reiterated these pledges even after he took his oath as President. Summed up, what these promises meant was: "Share our wealth."

When I saw him spending all his time of ease and recreation with the business partners of Mr. John D. Rockefeller, Jr., with such men as the Astors [heirs of John Jacob Astor, a

German immigrant who created a vast financial empire in America that began with his monopoly of the fur trade], etc., maybe I ought to have had better sense than to have believed he would ever break down their big fortunes to give enough to the masses to end poverty—maybe some will think me weak for ever believing it all, but millions of other people were fooled the same as myself. I was like a drowning man grabbing at a straw, I guess. The face and eyes, the hungry forms of mothers and children, the aching hearts of students denied education were before our eyes, and when Roosevelt promised, we jumped for that ray of hope.

So therefore I call upon the men and women of America to immediately join in our work and movement to share our wealth.

There are thousands of share-our-wealth societies organized in the United States now. We want 100,000 such societies formed for every nook and corner of this country— societies that will meet, talk, and work, all for the purpose that the great wealth and abundance of this great land that belongs to us may be shared and enjoyed by all of us.

We have nothing more for which we should ask the Lord. He has allowed this land to have too much of everything that humanity needs.

A Proposal to Share Our Wealth

So in this land of God's abundance we propose laws, viz.:

1. The fortunes of the multimillionaires and billionaires shall be reduced so that no one person shall own more than a few million dollars to the person. We would do this by a capital levy tax. On the first million that a man was worth, we would not impose any tax. We would say, "All right for your first million dollars, but after you get that rich you will have to start helping the balance of us." So we would not levy any capital levy tax on the first million one owned. But on the second million a man owns, we would tax that 1 percent, so that every year the man owned the second million dollars he would be taxed $10,000. On the third million we would impose a tax of 2 percent. On the fourth

million we would impose a tax of 4 percent. On the fifth million we would impose a tax of 8 percent. On the sixth million we would impose a tax of 16 percent. On the seventh million we would impose a tax of 32 percent. On the eighth million we would impose a tax of 64 percent; and on all over the eighth million we would impose a tax of 100 percent.

What this would mean is that the annual tax would bring the biggest fortune down to $3 or $4 million to the person because no one could pay taxes very long in the higher brackets. But $3 to $4 million is enough for any one person and his children and his children's children. We cannot allow one to have more than that because it would not leave enough for the balance to have something.

2. We propose to limit the amount any one man can earn in one year or inherit to $1 million to the person.

3. Now, by limiting the size of the fortunes and incomes of the big men, we will throw into the government Treasury the money and property from which we will care for the millions of people who have nothing; and with this money we will provide a home and the comforts of home, with such common conveniences as radio and automobile, for every family in America, free of debt.

4. We guarantee food and clothing and employment for everyone who should work by shortening the hours of labor to thirty hours per week, maybe less, and to eleven months per year, maybe less. We would have the hours shortened just so much as would give work to everybody to produce enough for everybody; and if we were to get them down to where they were too short, then we would lengthen them again. As long as all the people working can produce enough of automobiles, radios, homes, schools, and theaters for everyone to have that kind of comfort and convenience, then let us all have work to do and have that much of heaven on earth.

5. We would provide education at the expense of the states and the United States for every child, not only through grammar school and high school but through

to a college and vocational education. We would simply extend the Louisiana plan to apply to colleges and all people. Yes, we would have to build thousands of more colleges and employ 100,000 more teachers; but we have materials, men, and women who are ready and available for the work. Why have the right to a college education depend upon whether the father or mother is so well-to-do as to send a boy or girl to college? We would give every child the right to education and a living at birth.

6. We would give a pension to all persons above sixty years of age in an amount sufficient to support them in comfortable circumstances, excepting those who earn $1,000 per year or who are worth $10,000.

7. Until we could straighten things out—and we can straighten things out in two months under our program—we would grant a moratorium on all debts which people owe that they cannot pay.

A Feast for All

And now you have our program, none too big, none too little, but every man a king.

We owe debts in America today, public and private, amounting to $252 billion. That means that every child is born with a $2,000 debt tied around his neck to hold him down before he gets started. Then, on top of that, the wealth is locked in a vise owned by a few people. We propose that children shall be born in a land of opportunity, guaranteed a home, food, clothes, and the other things that make for living, including the right to education.

Our plan would injure no one. It would not stop us from having millionaires—it would increase them tenfold, because so many more people could make $1 million if they had the chance our plan gives them. Our plan would not break up big concerns. The only difference would be that maybe 10,000 people would own a concern instead of 10 people owning it.

But, my friends, unless we do share our wealth, unless we limit the size of the big man so as to give something to the little man, we can never have a happy or free people. God said so! He ordered it.

We have everything our people need. Too much of food, clothes, and houses—why not let all have their fill and lie down in the ease and comfort God has given us? Why not? Because a few own everything—the masses own nothing.

I wonder if any of you people who are listening to me were ever at a barbecue! We used to go there—sometimes 1,000 people or more. If there were 1,000 people, we would put enough meat and bread and everything else on the table for 1,000 people. Then everybody would be called and everyone would eat all they wanted. But suppose at one of these barbecues for 1,000 people that one man took 90 percent of the food and ran off with it and ate until he got sick and let the balance rot. Then 999 people would have only enough for 100 to eat and there would be many to starve because of the greed of just one person for something he couldn't eat himself.

Well, ladies and gentlemen, America, all the people of America, have been invited to a barbecue. God invited us all to come and eat and drink all we wanted. He smiled on our land and we grew crops of plenty to eat and wear. He showed us in the earth the iron and other things to make everything we wanted. He unfolded to us the secrets of science so that our work might be easy. God called: "Come to My feast."

Then what happened? Rockefeller, Morgan, and their crowd stepped up and took enough for 120 million people and left only enough for 5 million for all the other 125 million to eat. And so many millions must go hungry and without these good things God gave us unless we call on them to put some of it back.

Does America Need Another Plan?

Will Rogers

Will Rogers was an entertainer and writer who wove hu-
morous political commentary into his act and his writings. He dressed as a cowboy and represented the common man, often remembered for his claim that "All I
know is what I read in the newspaper."

Rogers conducted a weekly radio talk show, during
which his candid, rambling style, filled with pauses and
repetition, belied his attempt to get at the root of contemporary issues. In the following radio broadcast, aired on
April 28, 1935, Rogers reminds the listener of a previous
broadcast, in which he poked fun at all the "plans" the
government had come up with to solve America's economic problems. He had suggested that perhaps Americans had had enough of the government's plans. Rogers
points out, however, that so many plans had been hatched
in the week since his broadcast that it should be called
"Plan Week."

According to Rogers, one of the most ludicrous
plans of the previous week was Treasury secretary Henry
Morgenthau's plan to balance the budget by taxing the
estates of the rich upon their death. In order for Secretary Morgenthau's plan to be successful, says Rogers, the
wealthy must die on schedule, a sacrifice to which they
are not likely to agree. Rogers also questions what
Americans consider important by referring to their interest in the trials and tribulations of celebrities. He uses
the problem of accidents at railroad crossings to suggest
that Americans need to examine issues from all sides

Will Rogers, "Morgenthau's Plan," radio address, April 28, 1935. Reprinted by
permission of the Will Rogers Memorial Commission.

rather than either ignoring the problem, or worse, following one position blindly.

Less than four months after this broadcast, Rogers
died in a plane crash near Point Barrow, Alaska.

Thank you very much. We—we—we're here an hour
earlier today. It seems kind of funny to be . . . With
everybody advised to spend and the government
spending and everything, and then . . . It seems sort of funny
for somebody to save a little daylight nowadays. Put a little
of it on the budget or something.

Do you remember my act on the radio last Sunday night?
Well, even if you don't remember it, don't, I mean, it don't
matter very much. Fact is, I'd about forgot it myself. But as
well as I can remember it, I introduced a plan, it was a plan—
it was a plan to end all plans. That's what it was.

Well, it looks like it had the very—it had the very opposite effect. This last week has been one of the biggest plan
weeks I've known of in anything. It's the biggest plan week
the country has suffered in years—this last one. In fact, I
think they could have named it "Plan Week." Now one of
the big things that President Roosevelt made his original hit
with was when he said, "If I'm wrong, I'll be the first to admit it." So when I say we should end all plans, it looks like
I'm wrong and I'm the first to admit it.

So, it looks like we've got to have plans, and I've really
got to get busy on one, I won't give it to you today, but I'm
gonna dig one up. If you want a plan, brother, I can sure give
you one now. I presented facts and figures to show you that
plans didn't work. Now I did that last Sunday, see. Do you
think that discouraged the planners? Nope. Not on your life.
It just seemed to encourage them, looks like.

Dying to Balance the Budget

Right on top of my advice to not plan—well, there come a
plan from Secretary Morgenthau, who's Secretary of the
Treasury. His father used to be the Ambassador to Turkey,

and a fine old gentleman and a good friend of mine. But this Morgenthau, the young fellow, a very able man—he come out with a plan to put a bigger and better tax on these big estates, these tremendous big, an inheritance tax, it is, to be exact that is, on a man who died. And on an estate of say ten million dollars, why, the government will take just take about ninety percent of it, and then giving the offspring ten and . . . and . . . after Mr. Morgenthau gets through with him. And then on estates of a hundred—a hundred million and two hundred million, a billion, and—like that . . . well, well, the government just takes all of that and notifies the heirs. . . . Says, your father died a pauper here today. And he died a pauper here today, and he's being buried by the . . . let's see, it'd be MEBA, the MEBA, that is—the Millionaires' Emergency Burial Association. It's a kind of branch of the RFC [Reconstruction Finance Corporation].

Now mind you, mind you . . . I'm not telling all this—I don't hold any brief or any great grief either for a man that dies and leaves a million millions and hundreds of millions and billions. . . . I don't mean that. But I don't believe Mr. Morgenthau's plan will work, because he gives figures in there that shows what this new inheritance tax would bring in every year. He says—in 1936 we get so much, and 1938 . . . oh, right along, see. He gives these figures to show what it'd bring in every year—that is, as long as the Democrats stay in—and he seems to know—he seems to know just who's going to die each year. And how much they're going to leave. Now brother, that's planning, ain't it, when you can figure out that! Now suppose, now suppose for instance, he's got scheduled to die J.P. Morgan. He's got him scheduled to die on a certain year. And you can bet, if they can arrange it, they'll have him die while the Democrats are in . . . so . . . so they can get the benefit . . . so they get the benefit of that estate anyhow, see? Now, according to plans, J.P. Morgan, he's got to die in order for Mr., for Mr. Morgenthau to reach his quota for that year. Now while I think Mr. Morgan is a nice man—I never met him but once, that was a time when he was on trial in Washington and he had the midget on his knee and . . . I met him there, but he's a very nice fellow, very able, nice fellow . . . and I don't hear from him but very seldom. But I think his patriotism maybe would compare with some of the rest of us, but, but whether he'd be patriotic enough to want to die on this year scheduled or not—just to make Morgenthau's budget balance . . . I mean, I mean that's asking a good deal of a man to just die right off just so I can balance my budget. He might be rather unreasonable and not want to do it. As I say, old men is contrary—you know what I mean. And rich old men is awful contrary. They've had their own way so long that you can't . . . So in order for Mr. Morgenthau's plan to work out, I—well, I'd say if it's to work out a hundred percent he's got to bump these wealthy guys off, or something. Well, now, that's . . . the government's doing everything else but, you know, but there is a humane society, I mean.

Now a . . . you know, there was another—there was another big plan developed during the week. Did you read about Aimee McPherson [a popular evangelist], meeting Gandhi in India? Yes, yes, sir, Aimee met . . . Sister Aimee . . . she had a date with the Mahatma over there. Yes, she had a date with him. It was what the French call a . . . a rendezvous. I'd like to have had the talking movie rights to the conversation between Mahatma and Aimee. I'd of love to heard, heard, what they said, you know. I . . . I think the Mahatma wanted her to stay in India and help him with the untouchables, and Aimee says . . . Brother Mahatma, you ought to come to Hollywood, and, you know, and try and get near [Greta] Garbo, and meet some of our unapproachables[1] . . . and . . .

Well, speaking of plans, I will say this for old Huey [Long]. He didn't break out with any . . . He didn't hatch any new plans during the week. He's just settin' on the same eggs he was.[2]

And now a little later on, folks, I want to tell you . . . A little later on . . . To be exact, I think it's seven o'clock our time out here, and I guess that makes about four hours' dif-

---

1. Swedish-born, American film star Greta Garbo often avoided public appearances. Her legendary seclusion began in 1941 and lasted until her death in 1990.
2. Huey Long's "plan" to solve America's economic problems was to "Share Our Wealth" by taxing the income of multimillionaires and by limiting how much money anyone could make. This, Long believed, would ensure that everyone would have a guaranteed income.

ference—eleven hours in the East . . . oh well, you know what time it is. But tonight later on, the President of our United States is going to be on the air. He hasn't spoken to us since last September. He's spoke to a lot of people, but not us, I mean. And he must have something important to say because he don't just go shooting off every time he sees a microphone like these other candidates do. They can't pass a microphone without yowling in it.

And I don't know what he's going to talk about. Maybe he'll be talking about Mae West, everybody else is. In fact, I bet he'd rather talk about Mae than some of the things— some of the things that he'll feel obliged to talk on tonight. You could explain Mae's husbands easier than they could the NRA [National Recovery Act], I'll bet . . . and . . . You know, speaking of Mae, I'll bet there's nothing that would embarrass a successful person, you know, any more than having some old husbands show up on you at the wrong time. Just when she thought she had him in Brooklyn, he showed up.[3]

The President is liable to talk about catching fish off the Astors' [heirs of John Jacob Astor, a German immigrant who created a vast financial empire that began with his monopoly of the fur trade] yacht. . . . He's been down there, but I bet he don't talk on that, for he never did catch anything on that old tub. There's fish in the ocean, but that yacht gets theirs out of the fish market. They used to have photographers . . . remember, they used to have photographers, just they did nothing but just follow our presidents around just to get pictures of 'em when they fished, you know. Remember that? All around, just catching fish. Even Mr. [Calvin] Coolidge used to drag in a little inoffensive little perch now and again. Poor little fish—he'd drag him in just for the Sunday supplement. And Mr. [Herbert] Hoover would go out and hook some old mudcat for a hungry lens sometimes. But there's been three photographers starved to death during Roosevelt's administration waiting for this Astor's yacht to approach even a crawdad anywhere. They ought to put skis on that As-

---

3. Mae West was an American stage and film star whose frank sensuality and flippant good humor became her trademarks. West had seven husbands, and here Rogers refers to an incident in which one of West's previous husbands showed up on her wedding night.

tor yacht and go fur hunting. That's his racket . . . much obliged. You remember your history, don't you? You remember how some of our big estates were founded.

Planning in Washington

He might talk about the bonus,[4] the President might. He's kind of switched over on that. He has a plan of paying it. I never saw as many schemes put forward, you know. They want to pay it, all of them, the soldiers want to receive it, but it's just the way, everybody's got their own way and want to do it. I don't know how they can have so many different schemes when it's paying, it's paying the same bunch of men and the same bunch of money. Seems to me like they'll have to do with the bonus like we have to do with everything else now to get anybody to take it. They'll have to wrap it in cellophane.

But he may speak on that. And I'll touch lightly on it because I don't want to interfere with anything that he would say. Mine is just a—mine is just a little preliminary introductory remarks to his.

Of course, he's liable to touch on some of these new schemes to spend this five billion dollars. You can't you know, you can't spend five. . . . Now there's something you've got to have a plan for. You can't spend five billion dollars in the old-fashioned way. I'll bet you couldn't put a strong man in the treasury warehouse full of, full of hundred-dollar bills and give him a scoop shovel, and he couldn't shovel out that much money in the rest of his life, you know.

We used to . . . we couldn't spell a billion dollars, much less to realize it, or count it or anything. But we now—now we're a nation, we learn awful fast, and it won't be long now till we'll be working on the word trillion—trillion—that follows billion and then trillion. You'll read in the papers—Congress has just been asked to appropriate two trillion dollars to relieve the descendants of a race of people called Wall Streeters. The paper will go further on to say—this is a worthy cause and no doubt this small appropriation will be made, as these are descendants of a once-proud—proud—

4. The bonus was compensation promised to World War I veterans.

race—a once-proud race—and after all, they're wards of the government.

Getting Americans to Look Both Ways

Then they've got another plan, now they've got another plan. They've figured out that what's the matter with this country is—I'll bet you couldn't guess it in a million years. You couldn't guess this plan they've figured out what's the matter with the country, and they're going to spend a half a billion dollars on it. I'll bet you couldn't figure out what it is. Well, you know what it is? Well, it's that the people try to cross a railroad track without looking both ways. That's what it is. They're going to fix the grade crossings—that's what that is. Well, you'll say—well, the problem is to teach the people to look both ways. Drive up to the track and look up and down and then cross. Yes, well that's exactly what's the matter with, with us . . . even when, when it don't apply to railroad trains. Everybody's—everybody looks one way. In 1928 and '29, around there. That's when the train hit all of us, remember?[5] There wasn't a . . . there wasn't a soul—there wasn't a soul in the United States that looked both ways then. We certainly, now, now we've gone to the other extreme. We're so scared now that we drive up to the track and we won't do anything. We're just standing there. We just stand there and look, and look, and we won't cross the track at all. We even won't trust our own eyesight. If a train goes by and it looks like everything is O.K. and we might be able to cross, we won't do it. We're, we're so scared that we think it might turn around and come back and hit us again.

That's what the President is liable to talk on. It's to try to get us to quit standing there looking and shaking and being scared that something's going to happen to us. And he'll tell us it's the same, it's the same track, you know—it's the same old track, and the same . . . you know you've been crossing it for years, and all we have to do is just to use some judgment and carry on just as we have been for years. But we won't believe him. He's got to go to work—and now he's got to build

---

5. Rogers refers to the stock market crash of October 29, 1929.

a runway over the top of all these, of all these railroads—either over the top or under the bottom, and get that under there. To build it. They get that all done . . . of course, I think it's a good plan. Mind you, I'm not against it. I think it's a fine plan, and it will give a lot of people work and do a lot of things, although I don't think that it will do everything it is supposed to do. I don't think it will save all the lives, because I think this grade-crossing thing. . . . You'll just rush right over the grade crossing and right on down to the . . . and get hit at the first intersection by a bus. That's what you'll do. See? That's one thing about buses. You know, there's one thing about a bus—they're bigger than trains are now, and death is more certain with a bus when you get hit with that. There's no lingering illness with that at all. And the buses, and the buses come so much oftener than trains do anyhow, you know. A lot of times—a lot of times people have had to wait pretty near a day to get hit by a train—you know, you know they come so seldom, but buses are, you know, there's so many of them, why, you can just get hit pretty nearly any time. And I'll bet you never did read, too, of a, of a train ever hitting a car with just one person in it, just the driver in it, you know, just one lone passenger, nope. No, they just wait—they just wait till the car gets loaded, and then they hit everybody, and . . . Oh here, wait a minute. I ain't through yet. Now next Sunday I'm going to try and dig you up . . . I'm gonna have . . . If you want plans, brother, I've got one. Good night and thank you.

GREAT
SPEECHES
IN
HISTORY

A New Deal
for America

The Promise of a New Deal

Franklin Delano Roosevelt

Despite Herbert Hoover's experience, principles, and efficiency, Americans were looking for a strong paternal figure to lead them out of the depression. Hoover did not have the skills for dealing with people and the flair for politics that came naturally to Franklin Delano Roosevelt. While the economic depression damaged Hoover and the Republicans, Roosevelt's bold efforts to combat the depression while governor of New York enhanced his reputation. In 1932, Roosevelt won the nomination as the Democratic party candidate for president and, breaking with tradition, flew to Chicago to accept the nomination in person.

In the following address delivered on July 2, 1932, before the Democratic National Convention, Roosevelt pledged "a new deal for the American people." According to Roosevelt, the Republican and Democratic parties hold different views on the role of government in economic affairs. The Republican view that the prosperity of the few would trickle down to the remaining Americans has failed. Because big business ignored American workers and consumers in the early years of the depression, says Roosevelt, the federal government must now intervene with planned action to protect the welfare of all Americans.

Roosevelt campaigned energetically, calling for government intervention in the economy to provide relief, recovery, and reform. His activist approach and personal charm helped to defeat Hoover by 7 million votes in November 1932. Arguably no president before or since has

Franklin Delano Roosevelt, address to the Democratic National Convention, Chicago, Illinois, July 2, 1932.

pushed the role of the executive branch to its limits like
Roosevelt, who took on his paternal role openly and with
the support of the people.

T he great social phenomenon of this depression, unlike
others before it, is that it has produced but a few of
the disorderly manifestations that too often attend
upon such times.

Wild radicalism has made few converts, and the greatest
tribute that I can pay to my countrymen is that in these days
of crushing want there persists an orderly and hopeful spirit
on the part of the millions of our people who have suffered
so much. To fail to offer them a new chance is not only to be-
tray their hopes but to misunderstand their patience.

To meet by reaction that danger of radicalism is to invite
disaster. Reaction is no barrier to the radical. It is a challenge,
a provocation. The way to meet that danger is to offer a
workable program of reconstruction, and the party to offer
it is the party with clean hands.

This, and this only, is a proper protection against blind
reaction on the one hand and an improvised, hit-or-miss, ir-
responsible opportunism on the other.

Two Views of Government

There are two ways of viewing the Government's duty in
matters affecting economic and social life. The first sees to it
that a favored few are helped and hopes that some of their
prosperity will leak through, sift through, to labor, to the
farmer, to the small business man. That theory belongs to the
party of Toryism, and I had hoped that most of the Tories left
this country in 1776.

But it is not and never will be the theory of the Democratic Party. This is no time for fear, for reaction or for timid-
ity. Here and now I invite those nominal Republicans who
find that their conscience cannot be squared with the groping
and the failure of their party leaders to join hands with us;
here and now, in equal measure, I warn those nominal Dem-

ocrats who squint at the future with their faces turned toward the past, and who feel no responsibility to the demands of the new time, that they are out of step with their Party.

Yes, the people of this country want a genuine choice this year, not a choice between two names for the same reactionary doctrine. Ours must be a party of liberal thought, of planned action, of enlightened international outlook, and of the greatest good to the greatest number of our citizens.

Now it is inevitable—and the choice is that of the times—it is inevitable that the main issue of this campaign should revolve about the clear fact of our economic condition, a depression so deep that it is without precedent in modern history. It will not do merely to state, as do Republican leaders to explain their broken promises of continued inaction, that the depression is worldwide. That was not their explanation of the apparent prosperity of 1928. The people will not forget the claim made by them then that prosperity was only a domestic product manufactured by a Republican President and a Republican Congress. If they claim paternity for the one they cannot deny paternity for the other.

I cannot take up all the problems today. I want to touch on a few that are vital. Let us look a little at the recent history and the simple economics, the kind of economics that you and I and the average man and woman talk.

In the years before 1929 we know that this country had completed a vast cycle of building and inflation; for ten years we expanded on the theory of repairing the wastes of the War, but actually expanding far beyond that, and also beyond our natural and normal growth. Now it is worth remembering, and the cold figures of finance prove it, that during that time there was little or no drop in the prices that the consumer had to pay, although those same figures proved that the cost of production fell very greatly; corporate profit resulting from this period was enormous; at the same time little of that profit was devoted to the reduction of prices. The consumer was forgotten. Very little of it went into increased wages; the worker was forgotten, and by no means an adequate proportion was even paid out in dividends—the stockholder was forgotten.

And, incidentally, very little of it was taken by taxation to the beneficent Government of those years.

What was the result? Enormous corporate surpluses piled up—the most stupendous in history. Where, under the spell of delirious speculation, did those surpluses go? Let us talk economics that the figures prove and that we can understand. Why, they went chiefly in two directions: first, into new and unnecessary plants which now stand stark and idle; and second, into the call-money market of Wall Street, either directly by the corporations, or indirectly through the banks. Those are the facts. Why blink at them?

Then came the crash. You know the story. Surpluses invested in unnecessary plants became idle. Men lost their jobs; purchasing power dried up; banks became frightened and started calling loans. Those who had money were afraid to part with it. Credit contracted. Industry stopped. Commerce declined, and unemployment mounted.

And there we are today.

Unified by an Economic Problem

Translate that into human terms. See how the events of the past three years have come home to specific groups of people: first, the group dependent on industry; second, the group dependent on agriculture; third, and made up in large part of members of the first two groups, the people who are called "small investors and depositors." In fact, the strongest possible tie between the first two groups, agriculture and industry, is the fact that the savings and to a degree the security of both are tied together in that third group—the credit structure of the Nation.

Never in history have the interests of all the people been so united in a single economic problem. Picture to yourself, for instance, the great groups of property owned by millions of our citizens, represented by credits issued in the form of bonds and mortgages—Government bonds of all kinds, Federal, State, county, municipal; bonds of industrial companies, of utility companies; mortgages on real estate in farms and cities; and finally the vast investments of the Nation in the railroads. What is the measure of the security of each of those groups? We know well that in our complicated, inter-related credit structure if any one of these credit groups collapses they may all collapse. Danger to one is danger to all.

How, I ask, has the present Administration in Washington treated the interrelationship of these credit groups? The answer is clear: It has not recognized that interrelationship existed at all. Why, the Nation asks, has Washington failed to understand that all of these groups, each and every one, the top of the pyramid and the bottom of the pyramid, must be considered together, that each and every one of them is dependent on every other; each and every one of them affecting the whole financial fabric?

Statesmanship and vision, my friends, require relief to all at the same time.

Just one word or two on taxes, the taxes that all of us pay toward the cost of Government of all kinds.

I know something of taxes. For three long years I have been going up and down this country preaching that Government— Federal and State and local—costs too much. I shall not stop that preaching. As an immediate program of action we must abolish useless offices. We must eliminate unnecessary functions of Government—functions, in fact, that are not definitely essential to the continuance of Government. We must merge, we must consolidate subdivisions of Government, and, like the private citizen, give up luxuries which we can no longer afford.

By our example at Washington itself, we shall have the opportunity of pointing the way of economy to local government, for let us remember well that out of every tax dollar in the average State in this Nation, forty cents enter the treasury in Washington, D.C., ten or twelve cents only go to the State capitals, and forty-eight cents are consumed by the costs of local government in counties and cities and towns.

I propose to you, my friends, and through you, that Government of all kinds, big and little, be made solvent and that the example be set by the President of the United States and his Cabinet. . . .

And now one word about unemployment, and incidentally about agriculture. I have favored the use of certain types of public works as a further emergency means of stimulating employment and the issuance of bonds to pay for such public works, but I have pointed out that no economic end is served if we merely build without building for a necessary purpose. Such works, of course, should insofar as possible be self-sustaining if they are to be financed by the issuing of bonds. So as to spread the points of all kinds as widely as possible, we must take definite steps to shorten the working day and the working week.

Let us use common sense and business sense. Just as one example, we know that a very hopeful and immediate means of relief, both for the unemployed and for agriculture, will come from a wide plan of the converting of many millions of acres of marginal and unused land into timberland through reforestation. There are tens of millions of acres east of the Mississippi River alone in abandoned farms, in cut-over land, now growing up in worthless brush. Why, every European Nation has a definite land policy, and has had one for generations. We have none. Having none, we face a future of soil erosion and timber famine. It is clear that economic foresight and immediate employment march hand in hand in the call for the reforestation of these vast areas. In so doing, employment can be given to a million men. That is the kind of public work that is self-sustaining, and therefore capable of being financed by the issuance of bonds which are made secure by the fact that the growth of tremendous crops will provide adequate security for the investment.

Yes, I have a very definite program for providing employment by that means. I have done it, and I am doing it today in the State of New York. I know that the Democratic Party can do it successfully in the Nation. That will put men to work, and that is an example of the action that we are going to have.

Now as a further aid to agriculture, we know perfectly well—but have we come out and said so clearly and distinctly?—we should repeal immediately those provisions of law that compel the Federal Government to go into the market to purchase, to sell, to speculate in farm products in a futile attempt to reduce farm surpluses. And they are the people who are talking of keeping Government out of business. The practical way to help the farmer is by an arrangement that will, in addition to lightening some of the impoverishing burdens from his back, do something toward the reduction of the surpluses of staple commodities that hang on the market. It should be our aim to add to the world prices of staple products the amount of a reasonable tariff protection, to give agriculture the same protection that industry has today.

And in exchange for this immediately increased return I am sure that the farmers of this Nation would agree ultimately to such planning of their production as would reduce the surpluses and make it unnecessary in later years to depend on dumping those surpluses abroad in order to support domestic prices. That result has been accomplished in other Nations; why not in America, too? . . .

Rediscounting of farm mortgages under salutary restrictions must be expanded and should, in the future, be conditioned on the reduction of interest rates. Amortization payments, maturities should likewise in this crisis be extended before rediscount is permitted where the mortgagor is sorely pressed. That, my friends, is another example of practical, immediate relief: Action.

I aim to do the same thing, and it can be done, for the small home-owner in our cities and villages. We can lighten his burden and develop his purchasing power. Take away, my friends, that spectre of too high an interest rate. Take away that spectre of the due date just a short time away. Save homes; save homes for thousands of self-respecting families, and drive out that spectre of insecurity from our midst.

Out of all the tons of printed paper, out of all the hours of oratory, the recriminations, the defenses, the happy-thought plans in Washington and in every State, there emerges one great, simple, crystal-pure fact that during the past ten years a Nation of one hundred twenty million people has been led by the Republican leaders to erect an impregnable barbed wire entanglement around its borders through the instrumentality of tariffs which have isolated us from all the other human beings in all the rest of the round world. I accept that admirable tariff statement in the platform of this convention. It would protect American business and American labor. By our acts of the past we have invited and received the retaliation of other nations. I propose an invitation to them to forget the past, to sit at the table with us, as friends, and to plan with us for the restoration of the trade of the world.

Go into the home of the business man. He knows what the tariff has done for him. Go into the home of the factory worker. He knows why goods do not move. Go into the home of the farmer. He knows how the tariff has helped to ruin him.

At last our eyes are open. At last the American people are ready to acknowledge that Republican leadership was wrong and that the Democracy is right.

The Welfare of All

My program, of which I can only touch on these points, is based upon this simple moral principle: The welfare and the soundness of a nation depend first upon what the great mass of the people wish and need; and second, whether or not they are getting it.

What do the people of America want more than anything else? To my mind, they want two things: work, with all the moral and spiritual values that go with it; and with work, a reasonable measure of security—security for themselves and for their wives and children. Work and security—these are more than words. They are more than facts. They are the spiritual values, the true goal toward which our efforts of re-construction should lead. These are the values that this pro-gram is intended to gain; these are the values we have failed to achieve by the leadership we now have.

Our Republican leaders tell us economic laws—sacred, inviolable, unchangeable—cause panics which no one could prevent. But while they prate of economic laws, men and women are starving. We must lay hold of the fact that eco-nomic laws are not made by nature. They are made by hu-man beings.

Yes, when—not if—when we get the chance, the Federal Government will assume bold leadership in distress relief. For years Washington has alternated between putting its head in the sand and saying there is no large number of destitute people in our midst who need food and clothing, and then saying the State should take care of them, if there are. Instead of planning two and a half years ago to do what they are now trying to do, they kept putting it off from day to day, week to week, and month to month, until the conscience of America demanded action.

I say that while primary responsibility for relief rests with localities now, as ever, yet the Federal Government has always had and still has a continuing responsibility for the broader public welfare. It will soon fulfill that responsibility. . . .

One word more: Out of every crisis, every tribulation, every disaster, mankind rises with some share of greater knowledge, of higher decency, of purer purpose. Today we shall have come through a period of loose thinking, descending morals, an era of selfishness, among individual men and women and among nations. Blame not Governments alone for this. Blame ourselves in equal share. Let us be frank in acknowledgment of the truth that many amongst us have made obeisance to Mammon, that the profits of speculation, the easy road without toil, have lured us from the old barricades. To return to higher standards we must abandon the false prophets and seek new leaders of our own choosing.

Never before in modern history have the essential differences between the two major American parties stood out in such striking contrast as they do today. Republican leaders not only have failed in material things, they have failed in national vision, because in disaster they have held out no hope, they have pointed out no path for the people below to climb back to places of security and of safety in our American life.

Throughout the Nation men and women, forgotten in the political philosophy of the Government of the last years, look to us here for guidance and for more equitable opportunity to share in the distribution of national wealth.

On the farms, in the large metropolitan areas, in the smaller cities and in the villages, millions of our citizens cherish the hope that their old standards of living and of thought have not gone forever. Those millions cannot and shall not hope in vain.

I pledge you, I pledge myself, to a new deal for the American people. Let us all here assembled constitute ourselves prophets of a new order of competence and of courage. This is more than a political campaign; it is a call to arms. Give me your help, not to win votes alone, but to win in this crusade to restore America to its own people.

The Works Progress Administration: Relief for the Unemployed

Ellen S. Woodward

The daughter of a U.S. senator from Mississippi, Ellen S. Woodward was a state legislator before coming to Washington, D.C., where she became the second highest-ranking woman in the Roosevelt administration after secretary of labor Frances Perkins. Woodward, who directed women's work relief under three successive New Deal agencies, was the first southern woman to hold a top-ranking position in a federal administration. Although Americans had not yet recognized women as part of the workforce, Woodward's efforts to help poor women were considerable in view of American attitudes at that time. Woodward was an administrator for the Works Progress Administration, later serving on the Social Security Board. After the Board was abolished in 1946, she served with the Federal Security Agency until her retirement in 1954.

In the following address before the Democratic Women's Regional Conference for Southeastern States, Woodward reveals the extent of the problem of unemployment and explains how the Works Progress Administration (WPA) plans to provide work relief rather than direct relief for these unemployed Americans. Although direct relief is less expensive, says Woodward, many communities are unable to afford it; moreover, most Americans prefer work to the dole. In addition, says Woodward,

Ellen S. Woodward, address to the Democratic Women's Regional Conference for Southern States, Tampa, Florida, March 19, 1936.

WPA projects add to the nation's wealth and health: Putting people to work increases their purchasing power and work relief projects have helped build roads, hospitals, schools, recreational facilities, and more. According to Woodward, the Women's Division not only provides work for women but trains those without skills so that they might become employable. She concludes that as long as there is unemployment, relief should continue.

W hen I say that it is a privilege to be invited to address this large group of Southern Democratic women, I want you to believe that I am doing more than the banal and expected.

I am firmly convinced that the Presidential election in which you shortly will be engaged is one which will have far-reaching effects upon the happiness and welfare of a great number of our people. Naturally, I am heart and soul for the continuation of those policies which have brought this happiness and welfare about.

So when I express my gratitude to you, and to your chairman, Mrs. Hortense K. Wells, it is with the humble hope that what I have to say may provide you with a little additional powder and shot for the battles which lie before you.

The Problem of Unemployment

In the intensity of political opposition preceding the election, it is becoming more and more apparent that one of the most serious problems confronting the nation is being either distorted or evaded. That problem is unemployment—the question of the relief of the unemployed and the destitute.

To begin with, let us face the undeniable fact that unemployment did exist and still exists. According to the conservative estimate of the Committee on Economic Security, in March 1933, at the end of four years of an economic toboggan slide, there were 15,071,000 workers in this country cut off from their jobs.

And let us face the further and more painful realization

of what unemployment on so large a scale actually means to the country. Here we have no past experience to prepare our minds. True, in the last fifty years we have had periods of economic depression, what the economists attempt to explain away by calling cyclical depressions. Then, at the most a few millions of workers were idle, but always the country was growing—new processes and needs were developing and foreign markets were expanding. Under these conditions the pressure of demand quickly became so great that it broke through the stoppage.

But over 15,000,000, more than one-quarter of the workers of the country, were idle after four years of increasing unemployment, with no hope around the corner, no new frontiers, no new industry to supply a new general demand, such as the automobile, moving picture and electrical equipment had been in the past, and as a result of foreign tariff walls, not an expanding but a contracting foreign trade. This was no momentary situation, not just another cyclical "bad times." It was unemployment that meant mass poverty; a poverty such as our country had never met before. It meant a direct deprivation, a drastic lowering of the standards of living to approximately 36,100,000 persons.

These, we must remember, are not people living in distant Mongolia. They are not figments of the imagination called up by an hysterical government to disturb our peaceful slumber—they are actual American workers—your neighbors, my neighbors, people whom we pass daily on the city streets or meet in the village post office. No one can tell us they do not exist.

But this is exactly what is being done, not in clear words, perhaps, but by implication, either by ignoring their existence, or ignoring the problem resulting from their existence.

Now, it is a simple matter for anyone to criticize the relief program of the present Administration. It is simple, that is, so long as the critics ignore or evade the condition which makes necessary a relief program, but once we hold clearly in our minds a realization of both the necessity and the problem it gives rise to, most of the attacks upon Federal relief measures reveal themselves for what they are—vehicles designed to carry political ambitions.

Misplaced Blame

Again, there are some critics who admit the fact of a mass unemployment, but (and here also by implication) they would have us believe that the unemployed are worthless, shiftless human beings who are unwilling to work.

This last implication finds a far broader acceptance than realistic minded people imagine. There is a curious quirk in human character that makes it acceptable. The man who has a job, or the person who has some degree of security, is always ready to believe that the unemployed, the destitute, are inherently lazy, incompetent, and worthless. This is the traditional attitude. It began in the days when man himself was the tool who had to be employed ten, twelve, fourteen hours a day in order to produce the necessities of life. Today, with the machine replacing the man in factory, field, and office, millions of competent and ambitious workers are being forced into impoverished idleness. In spite of this obvious fact, the traditional attitude still finds many honest but unthinking followers.

Now, please don't misunderstand me, I am not placing all the blame on the machine. There are many other factors, we know, though a discussion of them here is outside my range.

But what I do want is to point out that even if President Roosevelt's Administration succeeds in overcoming all the other causes of poverty and distress in the country, there still remains technological unemployment.

This, in part of course, is due to the fact that some industry, rather than employ more labor, has lengthened hours of work and utilized the stretch-out system. It still means a mass poverty, destructive to the American standard of living. Obviously, therefore, more than a return of business to the 1929 peak is necessary to combat the continuance of mass poverty. And we may expect it to continue until America's capacity to produce and consume goods and services is graded up to a higher standard of living than any heretofore known.

The attitude of the Administration in attacking this problem comes closer to basic human values, I am sure, than does the traditional attitude.

The Administration is not willing to accept the implication that millions of American workers have suddenly lost all virility, all backbone, and all capacity; rather it assumes that human beings, that is, the general run of our average Americans, both those with jobs and those without, are made of the same salt. It assumes that in practically all cases the unemployed are victims of conditions over which the individual has no control.

In his message to Congress last year the President [Franklin D. Roosevelt], in introducing the Federal Work Program, said; "Work must be found for able-bodied but destitute workers. The Federal Government must and shall quit this business of relief. We must preserve not only the bodies of the unemployed from destitution, but also their self-respect, their self-reliance and courage and determination." With this pronouncement there was started a program which is today touching every city and village and reaching into the rural areas in every corner of this country.

Useful projects are in operation in every single State. About two months ago I made a trip across the United States from the East to the West Coast. I had the opportunity of seeing first-hand many of the projects in operation. It was a great experience, to see thousands of destitute but able-bodied men and women who have been removed from relief rolls and have been given an opportunity to work on useful projects at security wages. Every project had to be sponsored by a local or State tax-supported body before it could be operated. The projects represent, therefore, what communities wanted and asked for. In most instances the sponsors have furnished space, light, water, heat, and much of the materials used on projects. This is a cooperative arrangement between the communities and the Federal Government. The communities are delighted to take advantage of this opportunity not only to give employment to their needy, but to secure for their communities, through work relief labor, many necessary structures, services, and facilities which otherwise they would have to go without. In one city I visited I saw a project starting—I saw 800 needy women take off their hats and coats and go to work. In another city I stood nearby while 1,000 women received their first pay checks. It was good to see their faces brighten and their steps quicken as they went back to their places with pay checks carefully folded in their old worn purses—a guarantee of food, clothing, and shelter for their dependent families.

Work Projects Create National Wealth

Work relief is truly a recovery measure. Projects give work to the unemployed and at the some time add to the national wealth. To give public employment to workers when private employment has failed, is to translate into national possessions the energy that would otherwise be wasted. Not only are we helping the unemployed by giving them the one thing they want—*jobs*, but at the same time we are putting into their hands purchasing power which flows directly into commercial channels and starts the wheels of industry rolling. This, coupled with the purchase of materials and services necessary to conduct such a program, is a potent stimulus to business.

Now, granting that our unemployed are human beings, men and women who delight in life and the effective utilization of their energy, men and women beset only by that common human frailty which demands food, clothing, shelter, and a free play of social expression, the question then arises as to what is the best method of meeting that demand.

Here it is quite natural that there should be a diversity of opinion as to method—these various opinions analyzed reduce themselves to two, with which we are all familiar; namely, work relief and direct relief.

The Administration carefully weighed both methods. It was a free choice; there was no external pressure directed at or restricting it. Nothing compelled its choice other than what would be the better one for administering to human beings in need, and it chose finally and definitely the work relief method.

There is a precedent for this choice. When the depression clamped down on America and the bread lines began trailing out around the block, a number of municipalities, counties, and States recognized the loss in human energy and productive labor these idle workers represented. It was then that work relief measures were first adopted in this country. Unfortunately, so many of our political units were so close to bankruptcy themselves that work relief projects could not be undertaken on a scale in keeping with the demand. The local municipalities had in most cases exhausted their credit facilities and the contributions of private philanthropy were wholly inadequate.

There is also a precedent for work relief abroad. Practically all European countries adopted some form of work relief in meeting the unemployment crisis. Some of the public work programs are extensive. Much of the armament and preparation for war undertaken in foreign countries is actually a form of work relief.

I thank God, we have not had to adopt that expedient! It is noteworthy, however, that this form of public works expenditure frequently has the support of those who attack the constructive work program of the Administration.

In formulating the public works program, Congress and the Administration realized that work relief might give no more food, no more clothing, no more shelter to the needy than direct relief. It also realized that direct relief would cost less in immediate cash outlay. But it was convinced that in the long run direct relief would result in an irreparable loss of human and social values, and further, a loss of permanent and worth-while community benefits.

Our country, we must remember, was settled by builders and workers; what has been made of it in the past few hundred years is the result of vision, determination, and unrelenting toil. Still a young country, it is today the richest in the world, with resources and a productive capacity equaled by none, and noted above all for the energy and resourcefulness of its people. Are we to deny the quality and character of this country and of its people? Is the flow of energy of millions of American workers to be deflected into the stagnant, idle pool of dole?

The answer to these questions lies in the demand for work expressed by the unemployed themselves. They, the unemployed, have not yet given up belief in this country's future. To them it is still a land of promise, and they demand a hand in building that future.

The philosophy of the work relief program, therefore, is

based upon an appreciation of the true character of the American people.

Building Across America

Perhaps you would be interested to know something about the projects that have been carried on in our past program, now continuing under the Works Progress Administration. I will refer here to the record: Approximately 600,000 miles of roads have been built or repaired—mostly farm-to-market roads, which will enable the farmer to bring his products to market or mill at all seasons and at the most advantageous time, when prices are best. There are still some two million miles of dirt roads in poor condition upon which 65% of the farmers of America have to depend. Not only the farmers, but the mail carriers, school children, and farmers' wives will all benefit by the road-building program. Over 20,000 school buildings have been repaired or rebuilt. In the State of Wisconsin alone, 1,089 schools were overhauled and put into condition. More than 8,000 other public buildings have been built or repaired. Miles and miles of sewers have been laid and repaired. Practically all the State Capitols have been rehabilitated, and there is scarcely a county court-house in the country that has not been improved by our relief labor. Hundreds of parks and playgrounds, swimming pools, bath houses—all types of recreational facilities have been built. Approximately 2,000 miles of drainage ditches were dug, and 400 miles of streams were cleared, which resulted in drainage of hundreds of thousands of acres, in the campaign against malaria.

On January 1 [1936], there were 334 airport projects in operation in places where the relief loads are heavy and where large numbers of unskilled men must be put to work. This program is especially valuable, because the enormous increase in air traffic and the development of new fast planes make it doubly important from the standpoint of safety that there be more and better airports in America.

Several thousand tuberculosis patients were supplied with new hospitalization facilities. In Arizona an up-to-date tuberculosis sanitarium was built, and in many States additional cottages for patients were made possible through the work program. Approximately 1,000,000 bushels of seed oysters were planted along the Atlantic and Gulf coasts. Over 12,000,000 garments were made in our 6,000 women's sewing rooms, all of which were distributed to the unemployable on relief rolls. These sewing rooms gave employment to more than 150,000 women. More than 4,000,000 public library books were repaired last year and put back into use, giving employment to over 12,300 women and services to hundreds of thousands. Our library extension project carried on last year served over 1,000,000 persons and reached into the farthest rural sections of this country. Over 10,882 hot lunch projects in 41 States served warm food daily to 1,930,945 undernourished, needy children, which gave employment to 10,078 women from relief rolls. Other health projects in 45 States gave employment to 6,351 nurses who visited 3,532,841 homes and examined 2,015,993 children. A total of 89,410 physical defects were corrected for children.

I could go on for hours telling you about the worth-while accomplishments of the Federal Work Program, for there have been and are now thousands of excellent projects. Now you have probably heard a lot of unfavorable comments about the programs we have carried on, but despite the jibes about "boon-doggling," relief work in tangible, physical results, in cement, in steel and stone, in increased public health, educational, library and recreational facilities and resources, has added immeasurably to our national wealth. There is hardly a community in the country which does not bear the mark of improvement because of our work relief activities.

The Women's Division

But I must hurry along and talk more specifically about the women's program, since it is that program about which you and I are most concerned. There are two major functions of the Women's Division. The first is to develop and carry on in the various States work projects for eligible women on relief rolls—projects which are useful to the community and to the individual as well.

If a woman has a profession or trade, we endeavor to

place her on a project in her own field. If she is untrained but must make her own living, we try to give her training which will prepare her for some useful work.

The second function of the Women's Division is to see that employable women on relief rolls who are eligible for work receive equal consideration with men in this program.

I wonder whether the women in this country, and men too, realize just what the creation of the Women's Division in such a program signifies. It means the Administration is determined that women shall receive their fair share of work and that it has made special provision for the enforcement of that policy. When the President said that no able-bodied citizens were to be allowed to deteriorate on relief but must be given jobs, he meant women as well as men. Harry L. Hopkins, our Federal Administrator, has repeatedly stated that "needy women shall receive equal consideration with needy men." As evidence that this policy is being carried out, there was a study made about six or eight months ago, and it was found that at that time 53% of all the men who were eligible for work were working, and that 53% of all the women eligible for work were also working. At this particular time in the new program, approximately 65% of the employable women are now at work, and new projects are rapidly being put into operation to take care of the additional number who are eligible.

To fully appreciate the progress we are making, let's go back for a moment to the fall of 1933, when the Work Program for women started. There was no precedent to follow, for no program of the kind had ever been carried out in any country on a national basis. We had to carve out without chart our plans.

We have come a long way since then and are no longer novices at this business of putting women to work. Under the past program we were able to give employment to some 350,000 women. Under the present program the number is more than 100,000. The knowledge we gained from the last two years' experience has been of immeasurable value to us in planning for the present Work Program. We know who these people are now, where they live and in general what they can do or what they can be trained to do. We have learned that they represent some 250 different occupational classifications. We have learned to design projects which not only give women employment, but which increase their skill and keep them employable—so they will be ready to take advantage of the first opportunities for jobs in private industry.

The Problem of the Unskilled Woman

One of our greatest problems is the unskilled woman. Approximately 80% of the eligible women are untrained. My experience in this work for over two years makes me feel that we cannot stress too much the value and importance of training. On our own work relief projects the value of training has been proved.

The need has been so obvious and urgent that in every State, more or less spontaneously and simultaneously, training programs have been devised in conjunction with work projects. I know it will be pleasing to you to hear that though these courses differ in method and content, in every instance their underlying aim is that same education for living we all know to be fundamental to a bearable existence.

One especially well-worked-out training plan of this kind is in operation in Minneapolis, where a program of "Vocational Guidance" has been worked out, with the help of the Vocational Guidance Bureau at the University of Minnesota, for the benefit of 400 women, at work in a sewing room where sewing, garment making, dyeing, rug weaving, furniture repairing, etc., are carried on.

Three teachers are in charge of this training program; one being responsible for the subject of home-making, another for child care, and the third for all phases of self-improvement. Each teacher has one thirty-minute period a week for her subject; she may vary the program in any way she chooses, by outside speakers, by demonstrations, motion pictures, or dramatizations.

An additional hour every week is devoted to singing, games, and individual conferences in which the women may discuss their problems, their work records, and job possibilities.

The program has aroused the interest and support of the community and the women themselves are especially enthusiastic. Initiative and creative ability have been stimulated; home life and personal life have been enriched.

Re-Employment as a Result of Training

Since there has been such a decided up-turn in business, we have been receiving letters showing that many women who have improved their skills or learned new skills on our projects have recently gotten jobs. This is one of the most encouraging notes in our work relief situation. I have in my office a thick file of material labeled "Re-employment as the result of training." What it contains is a long list of names and addresses of women who have been employed on work relief projects. It tells what kind of work they did and describes the jobs they now hold in private industry.

The Women's Program, you must understand, is an integral part of the whole Work Program of the WPA. Throughout the history of its operation, a satisfying ratio has been maintained between the proportions of men and women employed, in relation to their numbers on the relief rolls. There has been no discrimination one way or the other. Probably the only distinction to be found is that training forms a more important part of our projects for women than is the case in projects for men. As I have already mentioned, a large proportion of our unemployed women are without skills of any kind. We hope, by training, to equip them for the jobs which are arising with ever-increasing frequency these days in private industry.

It is disheartening to many to realize that even in the face of our large expenditures for relief and the tangible signs of business recovery, unemployment itself continues a major problem. The financial pages of the papers are full of reports of increased earnings, increased dividends, increased orders, car loadings, and other unmistakable signs of a reviving economy. Yet in spite of these improvements, the latest reports on unemployment show the number to be still in excess of 10,000,000 people.

Critics of our program have used this fact to indicate a fundamental failure in our whole philosophy of relief. In so doing, however, they exhibit a sad lack of understanding. For there is a distinct difference between the problems of unemployment relief and unemployment itself. To state it more simply, unemployment is the condition which makes unemployment relief necessary. Obviously, to remove the necessity for unemployment relief we must first cure unemployment.

We in the Administration have been so absorbed in ministering to the imperative and insistent demands of a stricken people that we have not been able to give all the attention we would like to the causes of the ailment. Today, that has to some extent been ameliorated. There has been set up within the WPA a National Research Program, adequately staffed and financed, which is carrying on the most exhaustive study into the causes and effects of unemployment ever undertaken. When its findings are completed, I think we will have established some very definite signposts along the way to a solution of the problem.

Naturally, neither the WPA nor any other governmental department can effect the reforms that will be necessary to root this evil out. That is a problem for Congress. Such action undoubtedly will mean the revamping of our systems of production and consumption so as to bring them in closer relation; a more equitable distribution of the national wealth and purchasing power; and a spreading out of work opportunities to reach a greater number of our people.

These are reforms which all agree must come in time if suffering and poverty are not to remain with us. But until the time arrives—in the interim, while we seek the easiest and best means of effecting the change—there can be no let-down in our responsibility to those who suffer. Relief for the unemployed is a Government function which must continue for many years to come.

It is an obligation which will be met in a fearless and humane manner as long as Franklin Roosevelt occupies the White House.

The Agricultural Adjustment Act: Helping America's Farmers

Henry A. Wallace

Many consider Henry A. Wallace to be one of the most influential thinkers of the New Deal. Born on a farm outside Orient, Iowa, Wallace came from a family of farmers. His grandfather was the editor of *Iowa Homestead*, a journal of farming and rural life, and his father, Henry Cantwell Wallace, was the secretary of agriculture under President Warren G. Harding. Wallace was interested in the science of agriculture, developing the first commercially viable strain of hybrid corn. As the Great Depression worsened, however, Wallace turned from science to public policy, but by the time he became Franklin D. Roosevelt's secretary of agriculture in March of 1933, the American farmer was already in dire straits.

American farmers had been suffering since the end of World War I. During the war, the government had encouraged farmers to expand production and increase their yields, but at the end of the war, the demand plummeted, creating surpluses. Farmers found themselves in debt while facing shrinking markets, and many lost their farms. The economic collapse that followed the stock market crash of 1929 only added to their economic woes. Farming communities needed swift action. In 1933, Wallace, with Assistant Secretary Rexford Tugwell and others, developed the Agricultural Adjustment Act (AAA).

Henry A. Wallace, "Declaration of Interdependence," radio address, May 13, 1933.

The goal of the act was to "relieve the existing national economic emergency by increasing agricultural purchasing power." In the following radio address, Wallace defends the principles of the AAA. Hoping to raise farm prices by creating scarcity, the act authorized the federal government to pay cash subsidies to farmers who would reduce production. Wallace encourages farmers steeped in a tradition of rugged individualism to work together to cut production and restore rural prosperity.

Because farmers had already planted their crops before the act was passed, Wallace made the difficult decision to order the destruction of 10 million acres of cotton. Although this provided fodder for critics who opposed Roosevelt's New Deal legislation, it proved at the same time Wallace's determination to get surpluses under control. The AAA prospered until, in 1936, the Supreme Court ruled it unconstitutional; but Wallace was ready with the Soil Conservation and Domestic Allotment Act of 1936, which passed constitutional muster.

The new Farm Act signed by President Roosevelt yesterday comprises twenty-six pages of legal document, but the essence of it can be stated simply. It has three main parts. The word "adjustment" covers all three.

First, the administration is empowered to adjust farm production to effective demand as a means of restoring the farmer's purchasing power. The secretary of agriculture is charged to administer this adjustment and to direct, at the same time, an effort to reduce those wastes of distribution which now cause food to pile up, unused, while people go hungry a hundred miles away.

Second is an accompanying authorization to refinance and readjust farm mortgage payments. . . .

In the third part of the act, the power for controlled inflation is delegated to the President, and this too signifies adjustment—adjustment of currency and credit to our changed needs. My own responsibility, however, as secretary of agriculture is solely with the first part of the act.

It should be made plain at the outset that the new Farm Act initiates a program for a general advance in buying power, an advance that must extend throughout America, lightening the way of the people in city and country alike. We must lift urban buying power as we lift farm prices. The Farm Act must not be considered an isolated advance in a restricted sector; it is an important part of a large-scale, coordinated attack on the whole problem of depression.

Making It Work

If enough people will join in the wide and swift adjustments that this act proposes, we can make it work. I say *if* because this act is not a hand-out measure. It does provide new governmental machinery which can be used by all who labor to grow and to bring us food and fabrics, to organize, to put their businesses in order, and to make their way together out of a wilderness of economic desolation and waste.

But the machinery will not work itself. The farmers and the distributors of foodstuffs must use it and make it work. The government can help map lines of march and can see that the interest of no one group is advanced out of line with the interest of all. But government officials cannot and will not go out and work for private businesses. A farm is a private business; so is a farmers' cooperative; and so are all the great links in the food-distributing chain. Government men cannot and will not go out and plow down old trails for agriculture or build for the distributing industries new roads out of the woods. The growers, the processors, the carriers and sellers of food must do that for themselves.

Following trade agreements, openly and democratically arrived at, with the consumer at all times represented and protected from gouging, these industries must work out their own salvation. They must put an end to cutthroat competition and wasteful disorder. The Emergency Adjustment Act makes it lawful and practical for them to get together and do so. It provides for a control of production to accord with actual need and for an orderly distribution of essential supplies.

In the end, we envision programs of planned land use, and we must turn our thought to this end immediately; for many thousands of refugees from urban pinch and hunger are turning, with little or no guidance, to the land. A tragic number of city families are reoccupying abandoned farms, farms on which born farmers, skilled, patient, and accustomed to doing with very little, were unable to make a go of it. In consequence of this backflow there are now 32 million people on the farms of the United States, the greatest number ever recorded in our history. Some of those who have returned to farming will find their place there, but most of them, I fear, will not.

I look to a day when men and women will be able to do in the country the work that they have been accustomed to do in the city; a day when we shall have more industrial workers out in the open where there is room to live. I look to a decentralization of industry; and hope that out of this Adjustment Act will come, in time, a resettlement of America. But in this respect we shall have to make haste slowly. We do not need any more farmers out in the country now. We do need more people there with some other means of livelihood, buying, close at hand, farm products; enriching and making more various the life of our open-country and village communities.

Reducing Production

In adjusting our production of basic foods and fabrics, our first need is to plant and send to market less wheat, less cotton, less corn, fewer hogs, and less of other basic crops whereof already we have towering surpluses, with no immediate prospect of clearance beyond the sea. The act authorizes the secretary of agriculture to apply excise taxes on the processing of these products and to pay the money thus derived to farmers who agree to enter upon programs of planned production, and who abide by that agreement. There are increasing possibilities that by trade agreements we may be able on certain crops or livestock products to arrive at a balanced abundance without levying a tax on the product at any point. In no case will taxes be levied on products purchased for the unemployed.

What it amounts to is an advance toward higher prices all along the line. Current proposals for government cooperation with industry are really at one with this Farm Act. Unless we can get reemployment going, lengthen payrolls, and shorten breadlines, no effort to lift prices can last very long. Our first effort as to agriculture will be to seek markets and to adjust production downward, with safe margins to provide enough food for all. This effort we will continue until such time as diminishing stocks raise prices to a point where the farmer's buying power will be as high as it was in the prewar years, 1909 to 1914.

The reason that we chose that period is because the prices farmers got for their crops in those years and the prices they paid for manufactured goods and urban services most nearly approached an equitable relationship. There was thus a balance between our major producing groups. At that time there was not the terrific disparity between rural and urban purchasing power which now exists and which is choking the life out of all forms of American business.

We do not propose to reduce agricultural production schedules to a strictly domestic basis. Our foreign trade has dwindled to a mere trickle; but we still have some foreign customers for farm products; we want to keep that trade, if possible, and to get more foreign trade, if we can. The immediate job, as I see it now, is to organize American agriculture to reduce its output to domestic need, plus that amount which we can export at a profit. . . .

Changing World Conditions

The first sharp downward adjustment is necessary because during the past years we have defiantly refused to face an overwhelming reality. In consequence, changed world conditions bear down on us so heavily as to threaten our national life. In the years immediately before the war, our agriculture was tending toward a domestic basis of production. The war rushed us out upon the markets of the world. Fifty million acres of Europe, not counting Russia, went out of cultivation. Food prices rose. A new surge of pioneers strode forth upon those high and dusty plains once called the Great American Desert and found that they could grow wheat there. Throughout the country, sod was broken. America entered the war. American farmers stepped out to serve the nation as American boys stepped up in answer to the call. Before the surge was over, we had put to the plow a vast new area. To replace the 50 million lost acres of Europe, America had added 30 million acres to its tilled domain and thrown its whole farm plant into high gear. . . .

The oversupplied situation began as a result of the war. As early as 1920 American agriculture was served notice that martial adventures must be paid for afterward, through the nose. The agricultural deflation was well under way by 1923; half of Montana's wheat farmers had by that time lost their farms. In 1929, the agricultural deflation became a plunge. Today, agriculture is twice as much deflated as general industry; and its prices are down 40 percent below the level of prices in general.

Ever since 1920, hundreds of thousands of farm families have had to do without civilized goods and services which in normal times they were glad and eager to buy. Since 1929, millions of farm people have had to patch their garments, store their cars and tractors, deprive their children of educational opportunities, and cease, as farmers, to improve their practices and their property. They have been forced to let

During the depression, many farmers in the panhandle states were forced to migrate West in search of work.

their homes and other buildings stand bare and unpainted, eaten by time and the weather. They have been driven toward peasant, or less than peasant, standards; they have been forced to adopt frontier methods of bare sustenance at a time when in the old surging, unlimited sense of the word we have no longer a frontier.

When the farmer gets higher prices, he will start spending. He will have to. He needs things. He needs new shoes and clothing for all the family so that his children can go to school in any weather with dry feet, protected bodies, and a decent American feeling of equality and pride. . . .

To reorganize agriculture, cooperatively, democratically, so that the surplus lands on which men and women now are toiling, wasting their time, wearing out their lives to no good end shall be taken out of production—that is a tremendous task. The adjustment we seek calls, first of all, for a mental adjustment, a willing reversal of driving, pioneer opportunism and ungoverned laissez-faire. The ungoverned push of rugged individualism perhaps had an economic justification in the days when we had all the West to surge upon and conquer; but this country has filled up now and grown up. There are no more Indians to fight. No more land worth taking may be had for the grabbing. We must experience a change of mind and heart.

Facing New Challenges

The frontiers that challenge us now are of the mind and spirit. We must blaze new trails in scientific accomplishment, in the peaceful arts and industries. Above all, we must blaze new trails in the direction of a controlled economy, common sense, and social decency. . . .

This Farm Act differs from the partway attacks on the problems that have been launched in the past. This act provides for controlled production. Without that, no price-lifting effort can possibly work; because if there is no control of acreage, the better price increases the next year's planting and the greater harvest wrecks the price. . . .

Our immediate job is to decide what products to concentrate on, what methods of production adjustment to employ on them, to determine to what extent marketing agreements can be useful, and to appraise the necessity for and rates of processing taxes.

To help us in these determinations, as rapidly as possible, we shall have here in Washington representatives of agriculture and representatives of the processing and distributing trades. These men and women will take part in commodity conferences, and in the light of their technical knowledge will suggest which of the several plans of attack will work best for different crops and regions. Bearing their recommendations in mind, we shall decide just what action to take and when to take it. As each decision is made, we shall get it out directly and publicly to the farmers affected and launch organization efforts throughout the nation.

As President Roosevelt indicated at Topeka last September, the right sort of farm and national relief should encourage and strengthen farmer cooperation. I believe we have in this new law the right sort of stimulus to that end.

I want to say, finally, that unless, as we lift farm prices, we also unite to control production, this plan will not work for long. And the only way we can effectively control production for the long pull is for you farmers to organize, and stick, and do it yourselves. This act offers you promise of a balanced abundance, a shared prosperity, and a richer life. It will work if you will make it yours, and *make* it work.

I hope that you will come to feel in time, as I do now, that the rampageous individualist who signs up for adjustment and then tries to cheat is cheating not only the government but his neighbors. I hope that you will come to see in this act, as I do now, a Declaration of Interdependence; a recognition of our essential unity and of our absolute reliance one upon another.

Creating Opportunities for America's Youth

Aubrey Williams

Aubrey Williams, a social worker from Alabama, was a staunch advocate of programs for women and children, believing that the government had a role in promoting social justice. A protégé of Harry Hopkins, administrative head of the Works Progress Administration (WPA), Williams was selected as the national director of the National Youth Administration (NYA), established on June 26, 1935. The purpose of the NYA was to provide education, jobs, recreation, and counseling for youth between the ages of sixteen and twenty-five. The Student Aid Program paid students for working on campus, helping them stay in school during the depression. College students conducted research projects, served as departmental assistants, and worked in libraries or in the community, their earnings often making the difference between staying in school or dropping out. Williams also sought to promote racial equality. A fund was set aside to help promising African American graduate students. Approximately two hundred African American students received Ph.D.s during the 1930s compared with only forty-five between 1900 and 1930.

In the following speech given before a joint meeting of college and university administrators and secondary school officials on September 23, 1937, Williams describes the problems facing America's disadvantaged youth. According to Williams, the NYA was established

Excerpted from Aubrey Williams, "The College and High School Aid Program of the Youth Administration," address to the joint meeting of college and university administrators and secondary school officials, Harrisburg, Pennsylvania, September 23, 1937.

to provide young people who would otherwise not receive an education the money to obtain the food, shelter, and clothing necessary to attend school. The federal government will not dictate how school administrators should do their jobs, says Williams, but shares the responsibility of administering the program. The program is not designed to provide "easy money" but allows students to earn while they learn.

I am happy to join with you today in a discussion of the college and high school aid program of the Youth Administration for the coming winter. But before taking up immediate problems, I should like to speak briefly of the fundamental problems out of which the National Youth Administration grew.

The Problems Facing Young People

The Youth Administration was established to equalize opportunity for youth. It was set up to raise economically disadvantaged youth to within reach of opportunities denied them. It was a recognition by the Congress that there were large numbers of our young people to whom education, in high schools and colleges, was being denied. It was a facing of the problem that whole groups of our youths were caught in dead-ends and blind alleys with all entrances to an education or a job closed to them.

Obviously, in comparison to the millions of young people caught in these blind alleys the number that the Youth Administration has been able to help must seem small. Yet its total effects we believe outreach by far its grasp. The 650,000 youths it aided directly last year represents but a part of the effect it had upon the whole youth problem.

What is of more significance probably is the recognition by the government of the problems and dilemmas confronting millions of our young people.

Congress acknowledged when it established the Youth Administration that education must be more than free. For

there are millions who can only secure an education, particularly higher education, if some way is found to give the student a chance to earn some money with which to purchase
clothes, food, pay his rent, and otherwise to keep body, mind
and soul together. Education is still the privilege only of those
economically able to afford it.

The school and its opportunities have had no meaning
for millions of our young people. This was no fault of the
teacher nor the would-be pupil. It was the fault of our economic system. We know now that for education to really be
available for millions now denied it, that ways not now exis-
tent must be established by which food, shelter, clothing and
fuel can be obtained. This the National Youth Administration has done for a limited number. It has worked out a pattern. It has done for a few hundred thousand what ought to
be done for millions.

We enter this program of student aid this fall with new
problems confronting us. The fact that we have a smaller total sum of money for NYA purposes has made for many
tragedies—tragedies to able and aspiring young people. The
disappointment of those who have been turned down is of
great concern to this administration as well as to the schools.

On the other side of the picture, however, the upturn in
business and the improvement in the Nation's economic status has without doubt lessened the total need in this field. . . .

Sharing the Responsibility

It is my desire now to discuss with you briefly the administration of the school aid program. From the inception of the
first Federal work-aid to needy students which developed
within the framework of the Federal Emergency Relief Administration, we have insisted that its administration should
be shared in equally by those responsible to the Federal Government, and by those administratively responsible for the
schools attended by the students who were given work. It is
my belief that whatever success it has had is due in no small
way to this arrangement. In this mutually shared administration of the funds, we of the government have felt it necessary
to stipulate as a matter of national policy the general formula

setting the rules of eligibility, the average amounts of work to be [done], the methods of reporting and of payments, and some general proviso regarding character of work to be done.

But we have left the actual carrying out of these policies to the college and school authorities.

May I, at this time, venture to reinterpret the national viewpoint of the school work program with which I believe you are all fairly familiar. First, I should like to discuss the responsibility of the school and college authorities.

With the reductions in available funds in your institutions, this year as compared to last year, we appreciate the fact that your selections are all the more difficult. It, therefore, seems to us that we must develop some general procedures for selection of students with a view to developing uniform standards, retaining, however, proper regard for the requirements of the individual institutions. One poor selection causes more criticism and lack of approval of this whole program than satisfactory selection in a hundred cases. On this point I think we should take the position that any student who cannot demonstrate to the satisfaction of the most critical inquirer through the information filed on his application form that this aid is essential for his attendance at that school is not entitled to NYA aid. . . .

We have, this year, worked out a uniform national blank to be used in giving us information relative to your proposed work projects. From these work project statements we hope to be able to share with other schools the outstanding project plans and methods of administering the program. This is a pioneering venture. Almost every school has at least one or two unusual and socially desirable student aid work projects which afford a greater personal growth to the students and a finer contribution to the institution's needs in return for the money expended.

Looking at the Results

We have been delighted with the improvement of the work projects in schools this past year. Early in our administration we met the criticism that many of our students looked upon Federal aid as "easy money." This, as a matter of record, was never true, but it is gratifying that the most politically partisan now find little to criticize. As a matter of importance you and I know that the giving of work to students, both from the nature of the work and the character of its administration, has created a whole new set of values for the students assigned and the institution as a whole. There is considerable evidence that the attitude of the country generally is changing to one of sincere appreciation of this manner of giving students not only a chance for continuing their education but the opportunity to "learn while doing" and get practical experience in their fields of major interest.

For the purposes of the record, I should like to enumerate just a few examples of the work being done by students:

We took a sample in some 388 colleges. For the most part, projects upon which students were working fell into distinct types of work activities, such as: Research and Surveys, Community Service Projects, Ground and Building Maintenance, Departmental Service, Library Service, Clerical Projects, and Construction Projects.

This sampling of 388 colleges represented almost 24 percent of the total colleges which were participating in the program last year. The projects reported by them employed a total of 7,083 college aid students.

Under the Community Service classification were the following activities:

NYA college students served as directors of play activities and organized recreational programs and stunts at community playground areas, community centers, elementary schools, and high schools. City Recreation Departments, children's agencies, YMCA's, YWCA's, Settlement Houses, institutions for the blind, public schools, orphanages, hospitals for handicapped and crippled children, boys' clubs, Boy Scouts, community centers and churches were reported as cooperating agencies in supervising the students and in providing facilities for increased recreational programs to all young people in the community.

NYA students were assigned to teach and organize classes for out-of-school groups of youth and adults. These classes gave instruction in health, character education, academic subjects, handicrafts, dramatics, home economics, music, speech correction, etc. They were conducted in cooperation with the Emergency Education program of WPA, evening schools of colleges, CCC [Civilian Conservation Corps] camps, orphanages, hospitals, demonstration schools and churches. Instruction was given to crippled children, blind children, CCC boys, immigrants, illiterates, and provided an opportunity to many out-of-school youths and adults who wished to continue their education.

NYA students acted as assistants in public libraries and performed work in arranging special exhibits and displays; cataloguing and classifying books, data, and material of all kinds; performing clerical work in the libraries, shelving books, repairing and cleaning books; preparing special bibliographies; conducting story hours for children; and maintaining travelling library service.

NYA students assisted in investigations of delinquency and in guidance work with delinquent youth. They organized boys' clubs in those districts where delinquency was prevalent; they performed research and investigation of parole cases; made surveys of delinquency areas; gave assistance at psychiatric clinics and juvenile courts; visited families in delinquency areas, and families of paroled prisoners.

Public welfare assistance was given by NYA students working as aides to Red Cross in flood areas and giving assistance to local welfare agencies in the performance of the work of these agencies. The duties of the students ranged from clerical work to case work.

NYA students were assigned to work with civic organizations in producing community entertainments, concerts, plays, benefits, community singing, and free musical instruction.

In public museums NYA students were employed as guides and acted as assistants. NYA students assigned to ground and building maintenance projects were performing work activities on the college campus in ground beautification—tree surgery, removal and replanting of trees, landscaping and terracing. They assisted in the construction of swimming pools, tennis courts, observatories, amphitheatres, recreation rooms, adobe office buildings, bus garages, broadcasting units, retaining walls, sidewalks, roads, and drainage ditches. They assisted in the repair and manufacture of furniture and the repair of steps, floors and windows.

While a great deal of NYA project work is departmental, the following classifications represent student work which bears a close relationship to the curriculum of the department in the collection and preparation of classroom material and the expansion of departmental routine activities:

NYA students have collected and classified and prepared supplementary teaching materials for training schools; collected and filed classwork of students; arranged exhibitions of classroom work; acted as assistants in Teachers' Placement Bureau; assistants to faculty in taking roll and passing out material; were operators of motion picture machines for visual instruction; and assistants in training schools and grade schools.

In the departments of physics, geology, zoology, botany, metallurgy, and schools of medicine, museum models have been constructed—telescopes, tracing cabinets, specimen cases, sound equipment, mine models; students have repaired and assembled archeological specimens, invertebrates, fossils, zoological and botanical specimens.

NYA students assisted in research studies, made surveys in preparation for research work, prepared statistical tables, maps, charts, etc. This type of work is usually closely related to the student's major field of interest and has high educative value in the expansion and development of the student's experience in the application of classroom theory. Research work covered most of the fields of knowledge. I will cite a few of these projects to illustrate the work of NYA students:

They made occupational surveys and did special guidance investigation, and research in physiology, zoology and medicine.

These boys and girls did research surveys in the legal field; surveyed records of law students; made studies in property law; studies in merchant law; transcription of legal debates in foreign countries; compilations of social welfare laws; and compilations of insanity laws.

In psychological research, evaluations of test items and studies of culture cycles were made.

In economic research, studies of the social concept of money were made; industrial and business trends were followed.

Surveys were made of building illumination; of graduates

and their professions, salaries, etc.; community and delinquency surveys; surveys of Negro population; of student life; of traffic; and the use of food products.

In the field of statistics, maps, charts, and graphs were made, such as relief maps, historical maps, land maps, delinquency area maps, maps of game areas and weather maps.

NYA students assigned to work in college libraries performed a wide variety of services, such as, cataloguing, indexing, classifying and accessioning, binding and repairing books, clipping and cataloguing magazine and newspaper articles, typing and preparing reading lists and reference lists. These students also acted as circulation desk assistants and library departmental assistants.

The clerical type of project, as reported, included all types of stenographic and clerical assistance to departments, administrative offices, alumni offices, and information offices.

NYA students performing duties as laboratory assistants were given the responsibility of preparing laboratory materials; setting up laboratory demonstration equipment; classifying and identifying laboratory materials; making up solutions; and checking experiments.

I'm sure that with only this partial list of activities it is easy to see that there is literally no end to the possibilities for sound work assignments available in every institution. I have faith that every college head and every school superintendent and principal can, with a little initiative, develop a constantly improving program for real service both to the student and the institution or community.

Yours, too, is the sole responsibility for adequate and correct supervision. I appreciate the growing demands upon the administrators' and faculty members' time and energy, yet a project is no better than its supervision. Many excellent plans have failed because of poor or inadequate supervision. It seems to me that supervision of these projects will not and cannot be at its best until you as educators recognize the importance and possibilities of the Work Program, not as something extracurricular, but wholly curricular.

We have been discussing the school authorities' share of responsibility in the administration of the National Youth Administration's program and I confess that I find it difficult to leave the subject without yielding to the temptation so often succumbed to of going into what the schools and colleges ought to do about this whole business of education and the world outside. I shall, however, not yield to the temptation of counselling them, but I do hold that it is relevant to both the obligations and the opportunities of the Youth Administration to take this opportunity to discuss with you some questions that bear directly upon the relation of the National Youth Administration to the schools and colleges of the country as well as to industry and the world of agriculture and commerce.

First of all, I want to raise the general question as to the need and desirability of continuing the program of giving work to students as provided in the appropriations to the National Youth Administration. Granted that it was all right to do this sort of thing in the worst days of the depression, should it be continued now that better times have returned?

Second, does government assistance in the form extended to young people by the National Youth Administration tend to weaken rather than strengthen those youths that are helped?

Third, has the NYA student work assistance injected external controls in the affairs of the colleges and secondary schools of the nation?

With regard to the first of these questions, "Granted that it was all right to do this sort of thing in the worst days of the depression, should it be continued now that better times have returned?" The answer to this, it seems to me, rests on how far the general population participates or shares not only in the upward trends of business and agriculture but also, of more significance, how much they share in the total income of the nation. There can be no question but that we are in the midst of better times. Upwards of eight or nine million people have gone back to work. On all hands, we read of accelerated business activities. There can be no doubt but that men are making money again, but an examination of the spread of the national income indicates that there is, to just as great an extent as was true in 1929, large groups of people without adequate means even for bare subsistence. Moreover, as has been shown by several surveys recently conducted, a large percentage of families in America still receive

annual incomes which are considerably below a minimum
health and decency standard. The Bureau of Home Economics of the Department of Agriculture, in a series of studies
which it has been making of purchases made by families in
various communities through out the nation, tells us that in
1935–36 one out of four families in cities had incomes below
$750 and one out of three less than $1,000. In the small villages the situation was even worse. There, two out of five
families had incomes below $760 and more than one-half
had incomes below $1,000. Despite the prosperity which we
have achieved, if we consider the families of the unemployed
and those on relief, there are probably twice as many families receiving incomes below $500 now as did in 1929.

It is common knowledge that with 70 percent of our families having an annual income of under $1,500 that they do
not have any margin of funds with which to send their children to institutions of higher learning. So, the realities of the
situation are simply these: that unless the government or
some other means is found of aiding young people in 70 percent of our families, they have little or no chance to going to
college. Some measure of how great is the number of young
people denied even secondary school opportunities is indicated by the fact that the Census of 1930 shows that there
were 9,528,000 persons in the United States between the ages
of 14 and 17, while according to the United States Office of
Education, the total enrollment in public and private high
schools in the United States was 6,014,000, as of 1934, or
63.1 percent of the total. Here we see that 3,514,000 young
people in the United States were being denied attendance at
high schools. With regard to college, the figures show only
11 percent of those in the college age group—18 to 21—at-
tending any institutions of higher learning or 1,250,000 out
of 11,300,000. So we can come to only one conclusion and
that is that whether it be the National Youth Administration
or some other arrangement either within or without the government, if the spread of opportunities which has been begun
by the National Youth Administration is to continue, something must be provided which gives these young people—the
great army of wage earner families—a chance to earn their
way through colleges.

Making Young People Strong

With regard to whether or not the methods employed by the National Youth Administration tend to weaken rather than strengthen the moral fiber of our youth, that can only be answered fully by detailed following through of the youths who have taken advantage of these opportunities. Enough of the record, however, has been made already to indicate that not only has this thing tended to attract and give opportunities to young people who were strong, but it has left them indeed, if anything, stronger because of what they have done in connection with the National Youth Administration. For four years now those youths given work in the colleges of the nation by the National Youth Administration have been among those averaging the highest grades in their respective schools. . . .

As a matter of common knowledge, we do not have much to fear about this business of making softies of those young people who are eligible for work with the Youth Administration—they come from either families on relief or in such obviously hard-bitten circumstances that the daily provisioning of enough food, obtaining funds for the month's rent, and patching daily the clothes on their back, involves the whole family in the struggle.

Further, those who profess to be alarmed about the depletion of the moral fiber of our youth forget that we offer work, not a dole, to these young people. We do, and you should regard this as a youth work and employment program. From every college—from thousands of high schools—comes evidence supplied by the school people of the nation that not only are we not weakening youth—but to the contrary—by injecting the idea of work into the high schools and colleges of the country we have supplied a much needed and necessary element in the training of all young people.

With regard to the last question, "Has the NYA student work assistance injected external controls in the affairs of the colleges and secondary schools of the nation," let me say, I raise this question not because any responsible school official has within the year raised an accusing finger at us, but to again make our position clear. It has been our consistent position from the start that we would not ourselves, nor would we permit any of our local officers, seek to influence one iota the content of the curricula nor the administration of the schools or colleges. We submit that after two years we have proven our good faith, and I reaffirm that position for the future. The President in all of his instructions to me has made it clear that he wanted no efforts at influencing, or assumption of the duties or functions of, the schools or colleges of the country. And this we have done.

Our Future in America's Youth

Youth today, as always, seeks his place in the adult world. They want what all men want, homes, work, families, happiness. But youth, as with many adults, is bewildered. Even from the homes in better circumstances, youth is perplexed and shaken with a sense of insecurity. It has gone through the most trying period in our nation's history. It has lived out its childhood and adolescence in the years of the depression. Modern methods of communication and transportation have given it world perspective by removing local and provincial barriers. Green pastures beyond the home fence are as green to today's youth as they were to you and me or to our parents. Youth today is discerning, critical, and analytical. There is much evidence that youth today has accepted as its slogan, "Youth must share as well as serve." From an economic standpoint, the situation is much more hopeful than it was three years hence, but there is the recognition that recovery in industry, business, and commerce has not yet reached downward to better the position of the secondary wage earner in the average American family. Our program has helped, the CCC has helped, other federal and state programs have helped, but the problem has not been solved, the surface has been but scratched. The need is still far in excess of our combined efforts to meet the situation.

This leads to my closing observations on "What about tomorrow?" Because of my faith in the youth of America, a faith made stronger by the rigid tests to which youth has been subjected these past few years and from which youth has emerged rich in ability and integrity, I am convinced that from the ranks of these young people and the generations to come there will be developed in a greater degree the answers to the problems which we of this generation have been unable to provide, or which we have answered in error. Youth is finding a way out through its own leadership and the sympathetic and wise counsel of its elders. I am convinced that youth today through the youth of tomorrow will provide a more favorable and more wholesome atmosphere to pursue a richer and more fruitful life of service than we have experienced. Tomorrow will give greater attention to the well-being and happiness of the masses of men than to the development of material things. "This is Utopia," you say. No, it is merely progress toward the life more abundant. All this I believe possible but only if we do our part now, and our part is the leaving of no stone unturned which fails to give youth today every possible chance to learn, to acquire what is justly his, and to help him to serve.

GREAT
SPEECHES
IN
HISTORY

Labor Issues

Heeding the Voice of Labor

John L. Lewis

The son of a coal miner, John L. Lewis began working in coal mines at age sixteen, rising through the ranks of organized labor to become one of labor's most powerful leaders. His dynamic speeches swayed labor meetings from the time he began his service in the United Mine Workers of America (UMW) in 1909. In 1933, Lewis launched an organizing drive that rebuilt declining UMW membership. He also helped organize the Congress of Industrial Organizations (CIO), serving as its president from 1936 to 1940.

Under Lewis's leadership, the CIO led a series of strikes in the auto and steel industry. In 1935, at the General Motors plant in Flint, Michigan, strikers employed a new tactic by refusing to work while remaining in the plants. These "sit-down" strikes brought the plants to a standstill, and General Motors eventually gave in and recognized the United Auto Workers (UAW). In June 1937, the CIO sponsored strikes against steel companies that refused to recognize the union. Frustrated with the continued strife between labor and business, President Franklin D. Roosevelt remarked, "a plague on both your houses." Lewis, who had supported Roosevelt, believed this comment was directed at him personally and responded in the following radio address delivered in Washington, D.C., on Labor Day 1937.

In his address, Lewis insists that collective bargaining is an essential economic institution and claims that those who receive the support of labor should heed labor's

John L. Lewis, "Rights of Labor," radio address, Washington, D.C., September 3, 1937.

voice rather than speak against it. Many unions contributed to Democratic campaigns and, Lewis argues,
those who have made pledges to labor must keep them if
labor is to obtain its objectives peacefully.

The United States Chamber of Commerce, the National
Association of Manufacturers and similar groups representing industry and financial interests are rendering
a disservice to the American people in their attempts to frus-
trate the organization of labor and in their refusal to accept
collective bargaining as one of our economic institutions.

These groups are encouraging a systematic organization
under the sham pretext of local interests. They equip these vigilantes with tin hats, wooden clubs, gas masks and lethal
weapons and train them in the arts of brutality and oppression.

No tin hat brigade of goose-stepping vigilantes or bibble-
babbling mob of blackguarding and corporation-paid
scoundrels will prevent the onward march of labor, or divert
its purpose to play its natural and rational part in the development of the economic, political and social life of our nation.

Unionization, as opposed to communism, presupposes
the relation of employment; it is based upon the wage system
and it recognizes fully and unreservedly the institution of private property and the right to investment profit. It is upon
the fuller development of collective bargaining, the wider expansion of the labor movement, the increased influence of labor in our national councils, that the perpetuity of our democratic institutions must largely depend.

The organized workers of America, free in their industrial life, conscious partners in production, secure in their
homes and enjoying a decent standard of living, will prove
the finest bulwark against the intrusion of alien doctrines
of government.

Do those who have hatched this foolish cry of communism in the C.I.O. fear the increased influence of labor in our
democracy? Do they fear its influence will be cast on the side
of shorter hours, a better system of distributed employment,
better homes for the underprivileged, social security for the

aged, a fairer distribution of the national income?

Certainly the workers that are being organized want a voice in the determination of these objectives of social justice.

Certainly labor wants a fairer share in the national income. Assuredly labor wants a larger participation in increased productive efficiency. Obviously the population is entitled to participate in the fruits of the genius of our men of achievement in the field of the material sciences.

Labor has suffered just as our farm population has suffered from a viciously unequal distribution of the national income. In the exploitation of both classes of workers has been the source of panic and depression, and upon the economic welfare of both rests the best assurance of a sound and permanent prosperity.

Under the banner of the Committee for Industrial Organization American labor is on the march. Its objectives today are those it had in the beginning: to strive for the unionization of our unorganized millions of workers and for the acceptance of collective bargaining as a recognized American institution.

It seeks peace with the industrial world. It seeks cooperation and mutuality of effort with the agricultural popula-

When General Motors refused to recognize the United Automobile Workers (UAW) as a bargaining representative, members at an auto body plant in Cleveland staged a sit-down strike.

tion. It would avoid strikes. It would have its rights determined under the law by the peaceful negotiations and contract relationships that are supposed to characterize American commercial life.

Until an aroused public opinion demands that employers accept that rule, labor has no recourse but to surrender its rights or struggle for their realization with its own economic power.

The objectives of this movement are not political in a partisan sense. Yet it is true that a political party which seeks the support of labor and makes pledges of good faith to labor must, in equity and good conscience, keep that faith and redeem those pledges.

The spectacle of august and dignified members of Congress, servants of the people and agents of the Republic, skulking in hallways and closets, hiding their faces in a party caucus to prevent a quorum from acting upon a larger measure, is one that emphasizes the perfidy of politicians and blasts the confidence of labor's millions in politicians' promises and statesmen's vows.

Labor next year cannot avoid the necessity of a political assay of the work and deeds of its so-called friends and its political beneficiaries. It must determine who are its friends in the arena of politics as elsewhere. It feels that its cause is just and that its friends should not view its struggle with neutral detachment or intone constant criticism of its activities.

Those who chant their praises of democracy, but who lose no chance to drive their knives into labor's defenseless back, must feel the weight of labor's woe, even as its open adversaries must ever feel the thrust of labor's power.

Labor, like Israel, has many sorrows. Its women weep for their fallen and they lament for the future of the children of the race. It ill behooves one who has supped at labor's table and who has been sheltered in labor's house to curse with equal fervor and fine impartiality both labor and its adversaries when they become locked in deadly embrace.

I repeat that labor seeks peace and guarantees its own loyalty, but the voice of labor, insistent upon its rights, should not be annoying to the ears of justice nor offensive to the conscience of the American people.

The Problems of Southern Agricultural Workers

Aubrey Williams

In its zeal to carry out New Deal farm programs, the
Roosevelt administration inadvertently brought about
the eviction of thousands of southern sharecroppers, tenant farmers, and their families. The Agricultural Adjustment Act (AAA) of 1933 authorized the federal government to pay cash subsidies to farmers who would reduce
production, but government checks went to the plantation owners, not to the sharecroppers and tenants who
lived on the plantations and paid rent through the profits from their crops. When the government told farmers
to cut back production, sharecroppers and tenant farmers realized no profits and were forced off the land with
no way to support themselves.

In east Arkansas these tenant farmers realized that
the only way they could protect their interests was by
standing together. A handful of black and white farmers
met in a schoolhouse in Arkansas and formed the Southern Tenant Farmers' Union (STFU). This union was to become a powerful force in American labor. STFU cotton
pickers held a strike in the fall of 1935, and after ten
days, landlords gave in and were forced to raise wages.
However, in December of 1935, a landlord evicted one
hundred sharecroppers who could not pay rent under the
AAA restrictions. Because of the resulting STFU revolt, by
April 1936, Arkansas was making national headlines. The
STFU hoped for federal intervention, but not until 1938

Aubrey Williams, "Major Problems in the Rehabilitation of the South," address to
the Southern Tenant Farmers' Union and the United Cannery, Agricultural, Packing, and Allied Workers of America, Memphis, Tennessee, September 26, 1937.

did the government agree to send payments to sharecroppers and tenants. This provided little help, however, because landlords simply evicted their sharecroppers and
tenants and pocketed the AAA money for themselves.

In the following address given before the STFU and
the United Cannery, Agricultural, Packing, and Allied
Workers of America on September 26, 1937, Aubrey
Williams, a social worker from Alabama and deputy administrator of the Works Progress Administration, ex-
plores the problems faced by southern agricultural workers. Williams, who believed the government played an
important role in promoting social justice, discusses the
obstacles to changing these conditions including, for example, the institution of tenancy itself, which he claims
has strong connections to the institution of slavery. To
protect tenant farmers, says Williams, leases must be equitable and subject to some form of government or community oversight. According to Williams, a redistribution
of wealth in the South, as in the rest of the nation, would
promote prosperity for all Americans.

It is a great pleasure to be back in the South: I was born
and reared in the deep South, in the Black Belt of Alabama.
I think I understand its problems and its people, its wealth
of human material and deficiency of financial power and technical equipment, its possibilities and its limitations for making a distinctive contribution to American life.

I am happy that the occasion for my coming is this joint
meeting of the Southern Tenant Farmers' Union and the
United Cannery, Agricultural, Packing, and Allied Workers
of America. For I see in these organizations an effort to safeguard the interests of a large segment of the breadwinners of
the South and of the nation. A segment which, if not rein-
forced by organization and governmental assistance, is, in
some respects, the most insecure of any in the nation's economic fabric. If we understand security as embracing the
ability to make a living comparable to that of other workers,
a reasonable protection from ruinous fluctuations in this in-

come, and public services which insure a full social enjoyment of this income, then it is readily apparent that southern tenant farmers and farm laborers are among the most insecure of any of our national groups. An income of $300 as earned by tenants in 1934 is low enough but that was a relatively good year. What happens in years like 1932 and 1933 is heartbreaking. The recent study of incomes in the United States made by the National Industrial Conference Board shows six states in the Southeast with the lowest incomes in the nation, less than $250 per capita. When the states are ranked in respect to income from highest to lowest, twelve of the bottom fourteen states are in the South. But these are statewide averages held up by a few large incomes in the city. If the people in whom you are interested had $250 per capita, they would feel rich. In 1934 their incomes averaged $70 per capita. You are familiar with the tragic want that goes with these meagre and uncertain incomes.

It is one of the ambitions of this administration to combat such insecurity and poverty in all walks of life and in this respect the objectives of the administration are similar to those of your organizations.

I wish, in advance, to extend my congratulations to your organizations for the success you have already had in calling to the attention of the American public the manifest needs of the southern agricultural workers. Needs which have existed for a generation with little constructive effort to meet them. We all know of the efforts which have been made to thwart the organization of tenants and share croppers. The testimony of unimpeachable witnesses on this point is too strong. Anyone who takes the trouble to read the reports of your activities can hardly avoid a realization of the suffering which the leaders and members of the Southern Tenant Farmers Union have gone through to survive. The fact that you are meeting here today, after three years struggle, is evidence of your courage and determination and your belief in the justice of your cause.

It is well at the outset to take into account the difficulties and obstacles which mark every foot of the road towards greater security for those depending on agriculture for a living. To an audience such as this, whose daily life is agriculture, I feel a great hesitancy in attempting to speak on this subject for you know the details of the difficulties and the obstacles in a far more intimate way than I know them but it may be profitable for us, together, to review some of the major problems in the rehabilitation of the South.

In the first place, we have to remember that southern agriculture is an integral part of a national and a world agricultural economy and we have to recognize that as long as this is true, the South cannot lift itself by its own bootstraps but will be compelled to depend on the reconstruction of our national agriculture and the revitalization of our foreign trade.

At the peak of our relief load in 1935, there were more than a million families in the United States who had been dependent on agriculture but who had been so unsuccessful in weathering the depression that they had been compelled to seek public assistance. This number was on the relief rolls in a single month. It has been estimated that at one time or another during the depression some two million farm families have received relief. This gives us a measure of the insecurity of farmers throughout the nation.

The more we analyze this situation the more it becomes apparent that this was not primarily a phenomenon of the depression of the 1930s. Federal relief called attention to a numerous group of farmers and farm laborers whose distress arose from longtime factors, who had lived from hand to mouth for years before the financial depression, and for whom relief, the Works Program, and the Resettlement Administration offered the first opportunity to secure even the inadequate measure of living which these public agencies afforded. It is now known that agricultural depression began long before 1929 and that relative to industrial prices, agricultural prices began to decline soon after 1910. In addition, in many parts of the country, farmers had attempted to produce crops on soil which either should not have been brought under the plow or which has been mined until its fertility is lost. Soil erosion had been allowed to continue unchecked until over 150 million acres of land had lost all or most of its top soil. In some areas, farmers were attempting to make a living for large families on farms too small in size. In many sections, devotion to a single cash crop amounted to almost a worship of cotton, tobacco, corn, or wheat. More and more the practice of neglecting the production of food and feed crops spread, leaving the farmer vulnerable to the price fluctuations of a world market. A good many farmers also speculated in land values rather than farming their land, consequently, mortgage burdens accumulated rapidly. Opportunities for earning wages in off seasons were also dwindling as the timber, coal, and other minerals were progressively depleted in some areas.

Obstacles to Change

All of these disadvantages to agriculture operated more or less generally throughout the nation and in turn, had their effects in the South, but, in addition to all the other agricultural sore spots, the South had its peculiar institution of slavery; since the Civil War we have had the peculiar institution of tenancy, the direct lineal descendant of slavery. A map recently prepared by the Works Progress Administration shows a remarkable coincidence of the areas of heavy tenancy in 1930 with the areas of heavy slavery holding in 1860.

Again, I will not presume in an audience of this kind to engage in [reviewing problems] intimately associated with the tenant group. But I shall call attention to the fact that the handicaps of the tenant were not born of the depression, but were gradually evolved of a long-standing economic system and a firmly established pattern of social traditions and customs. Any institution which is so dependent on the world market, upon the national agricultural structure and which is so strongly entrenched will not be easily changed. I say this merely to encourage you not to weary in the face of obstacles and disappointments, for anyone who is endeavoring to promote such a fundamental change in society should be forewarned that these obstacles will appear and these disappointments will be met.

One further factor needs to be considered as contributing largely to the insecure position of southern labor, that is the pressure of population on resources. The increase in population of the country is now coming almost entirely from the nation's farms, especially since the stoppage of European immigration, and the southern farms are producing far more than their share of this natural increase. Of course, this increase of population has wide significance in social and institutional fields but we may confine ourselves at the present to its effects on the labor market. It means first that for every available farm there are several maturing farm boys and in periods of depression, when these boys do not move to the city, they compete for farm jobs in a glutted labor market. On the other hand, it means that when they do move to the city, they compete with industrial labor at a low wage level. It has been definitely shown that differential wages between the South and other sections of the country are greatest in those jobs which can be filled by unskilled farm boys and least in those jobs where a period of training or apprenticeship is necessary before the job can be performed. This emphasizes the interdependence of southern agriculture with southern industry and national industry. It tells us why industries owned by outside capital are locating in the South. They see in this mass of poverty a cheap and exploitable labor supply. The intelligent training and direction of these future laborers of the nation is a matter of gravest national concern and one not limited to the confines of the southern states.

I suppose, however, that you are not interested in hearing me recite the catalog of misfortunes with which you are already thoroughly familiar. I can see that the question which is uppermost in your mind is: What can be done about it?

Raising the Standard of Living

If the South is to achieve the place it so richly deserves in the national economy, its plane of living must be raised to a level which is more nearly compatible with standards of health and comfort for the masses elsewhere. It would be futile for anyone not a professional economist, statistician, political scientist, or social worker combined to try to map out a definite blueprint of how this can be done. There are, however, certain considerations which point the way. Considerations which revolve around changes in the basic economic structure. No amount of preaching of the gospel of hard work, of frugality, or rugged individualism will suffice to improve living conditions. Such improvement can result only from a concerted and determined effort on the part of southern workers, southern industry, and southern agriculture, aided by the federal government with the clear understanding that problems of the South are national in their effects.

The first, and one of the most obvious points of attack which is apparent to even the most superficial observers of southern agriculture, can be made on the credit system. No one in the South, be he tenant, banker, landlord, or merchant, is satisfied with the credit structure which drains so large a proportion of the South's farm income into the reservoirs of financial centers. It is the outcome of a vicious financial system which has fastened itself on the region, along with the devotion to the one crop cotton. The Rural Rehabilitation Division of F.E.R.A. [Federal Emergency Relief Administration], and later of the Resettlement Administration, has been able to make some headway in assuming risks which the commercial and the intermediate credit banks would not formerly assume for two reasons: (1) By making a large number of loans the risk has been spread over a great many sections and a great many clients, and (2) the loans have been accompanied by a type of supervision which the merchant or banker is not in a position to give to his borrower. In other words, the loan has been accompanied by advice and aid of the type most calculated to increase the income of the borrower, and thus, insure re-payment. This is obviously beginning at the right point, but only a beginning in proportion to the vast amount of high cost credit which is still used.

The most obvious method of raising the standard of living is to be expected from an increase in the effective incomes of the farmers. The Department of Agriculture and the State Experiment Stations have a number of programs in this field which need to be pressed to the limit. These range all the way from retirement of submarginal land to various devices designed to obtain parity prices for the farmers. Another method, and one which is less in the public mind, is in the line of reduction of costs of production and of marketing the product.

It is evident from the recent report of the National Resources Committee on Technological Trends that the technical improvements in agriculture are likely to continue at least as rapidly as they have in the past. It has been estimated that from 1870 to 1930, the output per agricultural worker increased from 100 to 150 percent. A similar increase per worker over the next 20 or 30 years would mean that the same agricultural production could be maintained with a reduction of 33 percent of the labor supply.

I would not, under any circumstances, oppose the reduction of farm costs by mechanization of crop production, but we must recognize that this is an existing trend and will bring with it the need for drastic adjustments in the labor supply and the demand for continuous vigilance on the part of those who are primarily interested in the human values in agriculture as opposed to cold production economics. Herein lies a challenge for all programs with a humanitarian viewpoint.

The Problems of Tenancy

If the level of living of some families is to be improved, it will be necessary not only to effect greater efficiency in the production of the total income, but also more equity in the distribution of that income. I am not of the school of thought which would assert that all landlords are overgreedy and grasping and too prone to exploit their labor. However, I know that owing to his lack of control of capital, his lack of education and experience, his poor bargaining position which is due largely to the pressure of population, and to his lack of prestige and political power, the southern farm worker is particularly vulnerable to exploitation unless protected by a strong public sentiment and social legislation. It is the function of labor organization and governmental regulation to provide this protection.

The improvement of landlord tenant leases is a field in which England is nearly 100 years ahead of this country, to such an extent that English operating farmers would for the most part prefer to be tenants rather than landlords, keeping their capital in livestock and machinery rather than in land. The general technique which they have adopted in this field has been the careful supervision of leases by local boards and the provision that improvements made in land

As a result of the Agricultural Adjustment Act of 1933, many sharecroppers and tenant farmers were forced off the land and left with no way to support themselves.

or buildings shall be paid for by the landlord when the tenant leaves the farm.

It is significant that the adoption of more equitable leases was one of the principal planks in the platform put forth by the President's Commission on Tenancy. It is of equal importance to an organization of this nature that the recommendation of this commission was directed entirely at the states and not at the federal government, since it was deemed impossible under the present constitutional limitations to promote a policy of federal control of farm leases. The adoption of any such program of improved leases by considerable proportion of the southern states, however, will depend upon the building of a far stronger and better organized public sentiment than now exists. Here is a task to which all people in organizations interested in the up-building of the South can devote themselves.

It may be too much to expect in the immediate future, but some of us present today may live to see wages and hours legislation, and unemployment insurance extended to agricultural workers. Other nations of the world, concerned lest their farm workers sink to the coolie level, have taken such steps and are well content with the results. It is not too much to hope that the future may add these bulwarks to the security of the American worker.

Improving Social Welfare

When we turn from the economic to the more purely social objectives of improvement in standards of living, we are immediately confronted with the present low levels of housing, diet, public health, and education of farm workers.

It is to be recognized that exactly the same type of house is not required in the South as is required in a colder climate, but the fact remains that whatever measure is applied, whether it be value of dwelling, number of rooms in relation to occupants, conveniences, such as piped water, sewering, or sanitation the shelter on cotton farms ranks below that of any large group in the country.

Similarly, the devotion to the one money crop has, to a ruinous degree, excluded the production of those articles which enrich the diet of more self-sustaining farmers. A glance at the *Southern Regional Study*, produced at the University of North Carolina, will provide ample evidence of the South's deficiencies in consumption of milk, meat, and green vegetables, and its devotion to pork, grits, and gravy.

There is no need to point out to a group of this kind that, associated with these deficiencies in housing and diet, we have high infant mortality and the almost peculiarly southern diseases of pellagra, malaria, and typhoid. It is indeed a scathing indictment of King Cotton that he has kept so many of his subjects ill-housed and ill-fed. It is high time that we demand an improvement in the welfare of the subjects.

A genuine and lasting improvement in the standard of living will not come without a genuine desire for a higher standard which in turn is dependent upon education and efficient financing of education and its sister, public health, depend upon the equalization of opportunity between the poor and the richer sections of the nation.

The guarantee of the minimum amount of education and of other public services consistent with the national interest is difficult without federal equalization between states because of the wide differentials in regional wealth and income.

Again the contrast is between rural and urban, agricultural and industrial wealth.

Redistributing Our Wealth

In addition, students of taxation agree that, with the integration of business and concentration of large incomes, it is practically impossible for a state which does not contain one of the large financial centers, to tax the wealth which is actually produced in the state and for that reason the broader tax base of the federal government should be used to collect from large surpluses and re-distribute to the sources of the actual production of true wealth.

The resulting inequalities in the tax base have placed six times more economic power per child in the richest state than is possessed by the poorest state and four times as much power in the richest quarter of our 48 states as there is in the poorest quarter.

This indicates that the inequalities in our state educational offering are not so much the result of a lack of interest in or of willingness to support schools but of an absolute inability to secure funds to provide opportunities comparable to the income receiving states of the industrial and financial areas.

We, therefore, have a condition where the states with the most rapid natural increase of population and the largest proportion of school children are those least able to support education by reason of the fact: first, that they depend so largely upon agriculture for income; and second, that so large a proportion of the income from their natural resources and from the processing of their agricultural products is collected and concentrated in other regions.

I wish today that we had a wider audience of people actively interested in raising the standard of living of the southern farm worker. For those outside the South, I would quote Booker Washington's famous aphorism, "You cannot hold a man in a ditch without staying there with him." The economy of the nation cannot hold so great a proportion of its population in the ditch of depressed agriculture without staying there with it.

For those professional people of the South and manufacturers and businessmen of the nation at large, I would call attention to the fact that when we say, "Raise the standard of living" we are, in fact, saying, "Increase the purchasing volume."

Southern farmers work in jeans overalls and for all too many of them, a pair of jeans overalls is all that they have to turn aside the sun and harsh weather. They work in brogans and for all too many, these coarse shoes must suffice for all occasions. Their children are often too naked to go to school. How much more pleasant would it be for the farmer, as well as profitable for the shoe and clothing merchants, if he could purchase an extra suit and pair of shoes for Sunday, and if his children could be fully and decently clothed. Likewise, it would be more profitable to the southern lawyers and doctors if they had good and steady paying clients. Also, increased spending power would make for the development of a dairy and cheese industry in the South and increased sales of processed foods.

In other words, there is no conflict between you who are attempting to form a cropper union, others who are forming textile unions, and the objectives of the New Deal, and the ultimate desires of the manufacturers and merchants who are in business for profit.

What I am trying to say is that there must be fundamental adjustments in the distribution of the national income if America is to march forward to a balanced progress instead of being strangled by the Epicurean excess of the privileged classes as were Egypt, Greece, and Rome. I am also stating that your job is a part of this redistribution process.

We had a national income of 80 billion dollars in 1929, but the distribution of that income was not such as to prevent a great deal of human insecurity and misery. This unbalance of income led to misery and want among the unemployed during the depression which in the past 5 years has run up a relief bill amounting to billions of dollars. This must not happen again. It is not unreasonable to apportion 8 or 10 billion dollars of an 80 billion dollar income as a preventative of want through the process of federal taxation and federal expenditure for smoothing out the unequal spots in our economic life.

The New Deal is merely a reflection of the growing conviction on the part of the American people that there is plenty for all and that all people can and should have a share in this plenty; that there is no reason for anyone in America to go without decent food, shelter, or clothing; that there is every reason why every last American should have some of the good things of life beyond mere food, shelter, and clothing.

Those who are opposed to this belief seem to fear that the process will take something away from them. We are not interested in taking away from anybody but are concerned that when we have prosperity we shall have balanced prosperity which will add some of the good things of life for those who now suffer in want. We believe that we should strive to see that future increases in the national income shall accumulate in the pockets of those who need the increase, not in the pockets of those whose land is already flowing with milk and honey, two cars, and numerous servants.

We are not only interested in more equitable redistribution of national income and the improvement of the standards of living of the lower tenth but we are also concerned with the democratic exercise of power.

Do not deceive yourselves. Efforts to set up such controls of power will meet with a blinding smoke screen of objections from the powerful. Prosperity, of a sort, has returned and those in power will endeavor to drug the workers with the doctrine that we should do nothing to endanger profits. But prosperity of the brand of 1929, where 36,000 families at the top had an aggregate income equal to that of 10 million families at the bottom is not the kind of prosperity in which the New Deal is interested. It is not the kind of prosperity which will make America permanently great.

The New Deal insists that if America is to be permanently great, its lawyers, its doctors, its merchants, its landowners, its bankers, and its laborers will unite on a policy of wide distribution of the benefits of prosperity and not on a policy of monopolistic control of profits.

More decent living standards for the southern tenant is an important part of this larger pattern of social justice—a part which is as essential to the up-building of America as it is to the up-building of the South.

CHAPTER

FOUR

The Arts
and
Education

Cultivating America's Interest in the Arts

Eleanor Roosevelt

Anna Eleanor Roosevelt was born on October 11, 1884, in New York City. She married her distant cousin, Franklin D. Roosevelt, on March 17, 1905, and was his helpmate throughout his political career. On March 6, 1933, Eleanor Roosevelt became the first wife of a president to hold a press conference, and she would deliver more than three hundred press conferences while first lady. She was candid, outspoken, and extremely articulate, motivating not only her husband's policy decisions, but popular opinion as well. Her participation in twentieth-century politics on issues from civil rights to international peace would have a lasting impact on the nation.

Eleanor Roosevelt was also an advocate for the arts, which is reflected in the following address before the Twenty-fifth Annual Convention of the American Federation of Arts in Washington, D.C., in May 1934. Eleanor Roosevelt claims that art, like nothing else, can express the American experience, and since the government began to support the arts, more Americans have come to appreciate the value of artistic expression. According to Eleanor Roosevelt, organizations like the American Federation of Arts can ensure that American artists are given the support needed to produce works of great beauty and national significance.

Eleanor Roosevelt, "The New Governmental Interest in the Arts," address to the Twenty-Fifth Annual Convention of the American Federation of Arts, Washington, D.C., May 1934.

I think that we all of us now are conscious of the fact that
the appreciation of beauty is something which is of vital
importance to us, but we are also conscious of the fact
that we are a young country, and we are a country that has
not had assurance always in its own taste. It seems to me,
however, that we are now developing an interest and an ability to really say when we like a thing—which is a great encouragement to those of us who think that we want to develop in a democracy a real feeling that each can have a love
of art, and appreciate that which appeals to him as an individual, and that he need not be afraid of saying when he
doesn't know a great deal: "Well, I like that, I may be able to
develop greater appreciation as I know more, but at least I
have reached a point where I know that I like this." I have
been tremendously impressed by the interest which has developed since art and the government are beginning to play with
each other. I have been interested in seeing the government
begin to take the attitude that they had responsibility toward
art, and toward artists. I have also been interested in the reaction of the artists to an opportunity to work for the government. I have had a number of letters, saying, "I have been
working on a government project. It is the first time that I
ever felt that I, as an artist, had any part in the government."
I think it is a wonderful thing for the government, and I think
it is a wonderful thing for the people—for the people of the
country in general—because through many of these projects I
think there are more people today throughout the country
conscious of the fact that expression—artistic expression—is
something which is of concern to every community.

Bringing Art to the People

Just a few days ago in talking with a rather varied group of
women, I found that those who came from other and older
countries had all been to the Corcoran Art Gallery to see the
exhibition there. Two of the Americans had been—but two
had not been, and one of them said she hadn't even heard
there was such a thing. Finally, they said that they would make
an effort to go, and one of the women who came from a country across the ocean replied, "But you must not miss it. It is

the most significant thing in Washington." I was very much interested that that should come to a group of American women from a foreigner. From my point of view, it is absolutely true, for in a way that exhibition expresses what many of us have felt in the last few years but could not possibly have either told or shown to anybody else. That is the great power of the artist, the power to make people hear and understand, through music and literature, or to paint something which we ordinary people feel but cannot reveal. That great gift is something which, if it is recognized, if it is given the support and the help and the recognition from people as a whole throughout this country, is going to mean an enormous amount in our development

Eleanor Roosevelt

as a people. So I feel that if we gain nothing else from these years of hard times, if we really have gained the acceptance of the fact that the government has an interest in the development of artistic expression, no matter how that expression comes and if we have been able to widen—even make a beginning in widening—the interest of the people as a whole in art, we have reaped a really golden harvest out of what many of us feel have been barren years. I hope that as we come out of the barren years, those of us who can will give all the impetus possible to keeping up this interest of the government, and of the people in art as a whole.

Fostering an Artistic Spirit

I hope that in all of our communities, as we go back to them, we will try to keep before the people the fact that it is money well spent to beautify one's city, to really have a beautiful public building. I could not help this afternoon, when my husband was giving a medal of the American Institute of Architects to a Swedish architect, thinking of the story which has been told by the government that he must finish this beautiful building in three years. When the three years were up he told them he couldn't finish it, that he must go on and take the time to really make it his ideal, the thing he had seen in his dreams—he did not like what he had done. And it was not the government officials who said, "Go ahead and make this thing as beautiful as you can make it"—it was the people of the country who insisted that if he wanted ten years, he should have ten years—and he should make of this thing something that really was the expression of a "love"—a piece of work that was done because he loved to do it.

That is something I hope someday we shall see over here, and that is what this Federation is fostering, I know. I hope that in every community throughout this country, that spirit can be fostered which makes a piece of work worthwhile because you love to do it, regardless of the time you put into it, and because it is worth everything that you can put into it to give to the world a really perfect thing. All that I can do tonight is to wish you all great success in the work that you are doing, and hope that those of us who are only learning and who need much teaching, will sometime be able to help you. Thank you.

The Time and Place for a New American Theater

Hallie Flanagan

Hallie Flanagan was a teacher and playwright who was well known for her efforts to relate theater to educational and social concerns. After returning from a tour of European theaters, Flanagan founded the Vassar Experimental Theater, where she used innovative techniques not only to restage classical dramas, but to illuminate social issues of the day. In 1935, Flanagan was appointed to head the Federal Theatre Project (FTP), which employed thousands of theater professionals who produced works seen by more than 25 million Americans. Flanagan is often remembered for the *Living Newspaper*, a series of documentary-like dramatizations of pressing social issues. Accused of promoting leftist ideas, Flanagan was brought before the U.S. House of Representatives Committee on Un-American Activities, which halted the activities of the FTP in 1939.

In the following speech delivered on October 5, 1935, in the national office of the FTP, located in the McLean mansion in Washington, D.C., Flanagan expresses her hope that with the help of the FTP, American theater will no longer be accessible only to the rich, but to all Americans. Rather than try to resuscitate classical theater, says Flanagan, American theater projects should reflect the rapidly changing world and shifting social order. Although one objective of the project is to employ theater people in need of work, Flanagan reassures her listeners that the FTP must seek quality rather than quantity.

Excerpted from Hallie Flanagan, "Is This the Time and Place?" address to the first national meeting of the regional directors of the Federal Theatre Project, Washington, D.C., October 5, 1935. Reprinted with permission.

This place in which we meet, at first glance so strangely inappropriate, becomes upon reflection one key to the situation, an epitome of one element in our American life which caused the situation.

Here we meet to discuss the problem of thousands of artists, no longer able to live in America except on charity; we meet to form a plan whereby people will again become enough interested in the work of artists to make such work a salable commodity. Behind us, hidden by a discreet panel, there is a carved wood serving table, imported from Italy, which cost $25,000. At the end of the hall, again cautiously veiled from the vandal or the irreverent, a buffet which cost $32,000. The hideousness of the chandeliers in the great ballroom, the busts and statues in the court, the gold faucets on the gigantic bathtubs, are only equaled by their excessive cost. In short, the McLean mansion, like many similar edifices throughout America, is a monument to the period of American culture in which the value of a work of art was measured in terms of its cost and the distance from which it was imported.

Irrespective of the merit of its art treasure, the McLean mansion represents the conception of art as a commodity to be purchased by the rich, possessed by the rich, and shared on occasional Wednesday evenings with the populace who, gaping in ecstasy, were allowed to file past the accumulated treasures.

The End of an Era

During the first days in this house I was haunted by a sense of having gone through this experience before; gradually that memory became focussed upon the golden palaces of Soviet Russia now turned into offices and orphans' homes and theatres for the Russian proletariat. I remembered a theatre meeting in the great Hall of Mirrors in Leningrad where reflected from every side in those mirrors which once gave back the image of the Empress, and later the execution of her officers, I saw the faces of [Joseph] Stalin, [Maksim Maksimovich] Litvinov, Lunachaisky, [Vladimir] Petrov and other leaders of political, educational and theatrical life. They met to discuss their mutual problem: how the theatre could serve in educating the people and in enriching their lives.

I do not at this time wish to press the parallel or to argue as to its prophetic implications. I merely wish to say that the present state of this house, with typewriters clicking where once musicians played in the long galleries, with out of work painters and sculptors carefully averting their eyes from various art atrocities while they ask Mr. Cahill for jobs, is characteristic of the decline of a certain period in American art and life. For it is not only bad collections which have had their day, but all collections. Holger Cahill, director of the federal art project, came to this job after several years spent in disposing of art collections of the Morgans, and the Rockefellers, for whom he had previously assembled such collections. Mr. Cahill also feels that with the passing of the private art collections one whole period of American culture ends. Personally I cannot work up any regret over the demise. That works of art in America today should belong in small collections to individuals who care about them and share them with their friends, or to the museums, which are doing an increasingly good job of making art intelligible and exciting to everybody, seems to me a very satisfactory state of affairs.

I only wish we had a method of play distribution as satisfactory: perhaps it is our job to find one.

Unfortunately the theatre, more than any of the arts, still clings to the skirts of the 19th century. A recent advertisement in *The Stage*, for example, read:

> The first ten rows are the people, the alert, challenging people whose opinion makes or breaks a play. These are the people who possess the gowns, the jewels, the furs, the country estates, the town cars—in short, all the appurtenances of fine living around which the smart world of the theatre revolves.

In the economic fallacy of such a statement lies one reason for the decline of the stage.

That the stage is in a decline is obvious. [Famed theatre manager and producer] Mr. Lee Shubert said the other day, with a bewilderment which I found rather touching,

> Once the stage was the dog, and the movies were the tail; now the movies are the dog, and we are the tail.

And who should know better than Lee Shubert?

That the decline of the stage is not entirely due to the economic depression is one of the basic facts which we must consider. For if we attempt to put people back to work in theatre enterprises which are defunct, we are engaged in temporarily reviving a corpse which will never be alive again.

A Time for Change

All the plans for reviving the road seem to me to be born of this naïve faith in resuscitation. Of course a great actress like Katharine Cornell touring the country in *Romeo and Juliet* will always have an audience; but the population of Oskaloosa, Iowa, or Fort Worth, Texas, is not going to be enraptured as in days of yore by a 3rd rate touring company in a mediocre play, just because such a company comes from New York. Oskaloosa and Fort Worth have been educated by the cinema and the radio. They know a hawk from a hand saw. They no longer measure art by the distance from which it was imported.

Our whole emphasis in the theatre enterprises which we are about to undertake should be on re-thinking rather than on remembering. The good old days may have been very good days indeed, but they are gone. New days are upon us and the plays that we do and the ways that we do them should be informed by our consciousness of the art and economies of 1935.

We live in a changing world: man is whispering through space, soaring to the stars in ships, flinging miles of steel and glass into the air. Shall the theatre continue to huddle in the confines of a painted box? The movies, in their kaleidoscopic speed and juxtaposition of external objects and internal emotions, are seeking to find visible and audible expression for the tempo and the psychology of our time. The stage too must experiment—with ideas, with psychological relationship of men and women, with speech and rhythm forms, with dance and movement, with color and light—or it must—and should—become a museum product.

In an age of terrific implications as to wealth and poverty, as to the functions of government, as to peace and war, as to the relation of the artist to all these forces, the theatre must grow up. The theatre must become conscious of the implications of the changing social order, or the changing social order will ignore, and rightly, the implications of the theatre.

Strategically, we are in a very fortunate position. Our liabilities, as is so often the case in life and art, are our assets. For we cannot subsidize existing theatrical enterprises, however excellent. The more fools we, then, if we model our new enterprises in the image of those now appealing to us for help. We cannot afford vast expenditures for scenery and costumes; another advantage, for scenery and costumes as we very well know have become too often the dog wagging the tail. We have plenty of designers—137 on relief rolls in New York City—we have a good many spot lights, and we have 250,000 yards of plain ticking in the government's surplus commodities; the result ought to be something pretty good, without benefit of Bergdorf-Goodman.

Putting Artists to Work

We should not be fatuous enough, however, to think that it will all be beer and skittles. If we have 6,000 theatre people on relief we all know that probably 4,000 of them are not of the calibre to experiment. However, we must keep steadily in mind that we do not work with the 6,000 alone. We work also with the 600 whom we may choose to work with them; and with the 300 whom we choose to direct them; and with as many apprentices as we can absorb from the National Youth Administration, who are ready and willing to pay underprivileged youths from 16 to 25 for studying with the various art groups.

Let us not, therefore, over emphasize the weaknesses of the material with which we work. Mr. [Harry] Hopkins, in his last talk with the directors of the various art projects before he left on the western trip with President [Franklin D.] Roosevelt, reemphasized his position: that it was quality rather than quantity which was to be the keynote of the art program. He reaffirmed that we were to turn back to the employment service people who had no chance of making a living through the theatre after this project ends. That we were to bend our energies toward creating theatre units which would be so vital to community needs that they would continue to function after our funds are withdrawn. Our best efforts must be spent in finding intelligent and imaginative theatre plans, excellent direction and adequate sponsorship for such plans. . . .

The focus of most of the discussion during today and tomorrow will center, rightly, on how the theatre project can help the unemployed. Underneath this, however, let us continue to think how it can help the theatre.

In a play, *My County Right or Left*, written by college students and produced on a college stage, there was a scene in which an intellectual, walking alone, philosophizing about art, is confronted by a woman who emerges from a motionless crowd of workers in the background.

The worker woman says, "Is this the appointed hour? Is this the time and place where we should meet?"

The intellectual, removing his hat, remarks cautiously,

"I do not think that we have met before."

To which the worker woman replies,

"I've walked the world for six years. I've noticed you. I knew that someday you would notice me."

Is it too much to think that, for two great forces, mutually in need of each other, the federal theatre project of 1935 may be the appointed time and place?

Education and Social Responsibility

Robert Maynard Hutchins

Robert Maynard Hutchins was born in Brooklyn, New York, in 1899 and earned his law degree from Yale, eventually becoming the school's dean. However, it was while president of the University of Chicago that Hutchins made a name as an educational innovator. Hutchins encouraged the admission of high school students before their graduation and the establishment of a four-year, "junior" college and liberal arts university separate from the university's graduate/professional schools. Hutchins hoped to bolster undergraduate education, believing that education was essential to the success of democratic principles. Hutchins wrote many books including *The Higher Learning of America*, *Education for Freedom*, and *Morals, Religion, and Higher Education.*

In the following address delivered before the Annual Meeting of the American Council on Education in Washington, D.C., on May 7, 1938, Hutchins expresses his belief in the relationship between education and the improvement of society. According to Hutchins, in order for students to develop a sense of social responsibility, they must learn to "think straight." To do so, Hutchins urges that all students study history and philosophy. Hutchins argues that it is dangerous to depend on political and economic leaders who act on feelings rather than thought; the nation must produce more educated leaders who can improve society and will want to do so.

Robert Maynard Hutchins, "Education and Social Movements," address to the Annual Meeting of the American Council on Education, Washington, D.C., May 7, 1938.

I should like this afternoon to try to make one simple point. I should like to show the relation between education and the improvement of society. We all want to improve society, and we want college graduates because of their education to want to improve society and to know how to do it. Differences appear when we come to the method by which these educational objects may be attained. I shall not attempt to deal with the problem of how a university may through its scientific investigations best prevent or cure soil erosion, juvenile delinquency, or the current depression. I shall discuss only the method by which an institution may through its educational efforts develop in its students a social consciousness and a social conscience.

At first glance it would seem that we should all agree that in order to talk about society or its improvement we should have to inquire into the nature of society, into the common and abiding characteristics of society, and of those unusual animals who compose it, namely, men. We should want to consider the history of societies, their rise, development, and decay. We should wish to examine their object, the various ways of achieving it, and the degree to which each succeeded or failed. In order to talk about success or failure we should have to have some notions about what a good society was. Without such notions we could not appraise the societies that came under our eye or the one in which we lived. We should need to have some conception of a good society in order to decide what improvement was; for we all know that we have welcomed many measures as beneficent which when adopted have seemed to leave us in as unsatisfactory condition as we were before. In short, if we approached the great task of improving society without prejudice, we should think at once of trying to understand the nature, the purpose, and the history of the institutions which man has created. The quest for social improvement is a perpetual quest. Ever since societies existed men have been trying to make them better. The ideas and the experience of mankind should, one would think, be placed in the hands of the rising generation as it goes forward on the perpetual quest.

This would mean that if we wanted to give a student a sense of social responsibility and the desire to live up to his obligations we should have to give him for this purpose whatever we gave him for other purposes, an education in history and philosophy, together with the disciplines needed to understand those fields. For the purpose of making him an improver of society we should hope to make him master of the political wisdom of the race. Without it he could not understand a social problem. He could not criticize a social institution. He would be without the weapons needed to attack or to defend one. He could not tell a good one from a bad one. He could not think intelligently about one. Even politicians seem to have gained an inkling of this truth; for Governor La Follette[1] said ten days ago that the country has failed to meet the problems of the depression because "we have not done better thinking. Before we can act straight," he said, "we must first think straight."

It is hardly necessary for me to add that nobody can think straight about a practical problem like the problem of improving society unless he knows the facts. He cannot comment usefully on the situation in Germany unless he knows what the situation is. Neither can he do so unless he has some standard of criticism and of action. This standard cannot, of course, be a mathematical formula or some miraculous automatic intellectual gadget which when applied to the facts will immediately and infallibly produce the right answer. The practical world is a world of contingent singular things and not a mathematical system. No one has emphasized this point more forcibly than Aristotle. But this did not restrain him from attempting in the *Ethics* and *Politics* to work out the general principles of the good life and the good state, or from trying to show the utility of such principles, with due allowance for changes in circumstances, in his society, and, as I think, in any other.

If, then, we are to have standards of social criticism and social action, and if they are to be anything but emotional standards, they must result from philosophical and historical study and from the habit of straight thinking therein. It would be a wonderful thing if we were all so conditioned

1. Philip La Follette, governor of Wisconsin and son of Robert M. La Follette, a nationally known Progressive of the first quarter of the twentieth century

that our reflexes worked unanimously in the right direction when confronted by political and economic injustice, if we could be trained in infancy to recognize and fight it. But even if we could arrive at adolescence in this happy state I am afraid that our excellent habits might fall away under pressure. Something is needed to preserve them, and this is understanding. This is another way of saying that the intellect commands the will. Our parents should make every effort in our childhood to moderate our passions and to habituate us to justice and prudence. But the role of higher education in this connection must be to supply the firm and enduring groundwork to sustain these habits when the tumult of adult life beats upon them.

The Four Cults of Opposition

It seems obvious to me, therefore, that the kind of education that I have been urging is the kind that helps to develop a social consciousness and a social conscience. Why isn't it obvious to everybody else? The first reason, I think, is the popularity of the cult of skepticism. I have been saying that I want to give the student knowledge about society. But we have got ourselves into such a state of mind that if anybody outside of natural science says he knows anything, he is a dogmatist, an authoritarian, a reactionary, and a fascist. Anybody who says, "I don't know because nobody can"; or, "Everything is a matter of opinion"; or, "I will take no position because I am tolerant and open-minded" is a liberal, progressive, democratic fellow to whom the fate of the world may safely be entrusted. All philosophical knowledge of society is superstition. All superstitions hinder progress. Therefore all philosophical knowledge of society hinders the progress of society.

I regret that I am forced to remind you that the two most eminent skeptics of modern times were among its most stalwart reactionaries. [David] Hume was a Tory of the deepest dye, and [Michel de] Montaigne was, too. This was a perfectly natural consequence of their philosophical position. Montaigne held, in effect, that

> . . . there was nothing more dangerous than to touch a political order once it had been established. For who knows

whether the next will be better? The world is living by custom and tradition; we should not disturb it on the strength of private opinions which express little more than our own moods and humors, or, at the utmost, the local prejudices of our own country.

The decision to which the skepticism of Hume and Montaigne led them was the decision to let the world alone. There is another decision to which they could have come and at which others of their faith have actually arrived. If we can know nothing about society, if we can have only opinion about it, and if one man's opinion is as good as another's, then we may decide to get what we irrationally want by the use of irrational means, namely, force. The appeal to reason is vain in a skeptical world. That appeal can only be successful if those appealed to have some rational views of the society of which they are a part.

A second reason why some people doubt the social utility of the education I favor is that they belong to the cult of immediacy, or of what may be called presentism. In this view the way to comprehend the world is to grapple with the reality you find about you. You tour the stockyards and the steel plants and understand the industrial system. There is no past. Any reference to antiquity or the Middle Ages shows that you are not interested in social progress. Philosophy is merely a function of its time and place. We live in a different time and usually a different place. Hence philosophers who lived yesterday have nothing to say to us today.

But we cannot understand the environment by looking at it. It presents itself to us as a mass of incomprehensible items. Simply collecting these items does not enlighten us. It may lead only to that worship of information which, according to John Dewey, still curses the social studies, and understanding escapes us still. We attack old problems not knowing they are old and make the same mistakes because we do not know they were made. So today Stuart Chase and Thurman Arnold, those great discoverers, are renewing the mediaeval controversy between the nominalists and the realists without realizing that the subject was ever discussed before and without the knowledge or training to conduct the discussion to any intelligible end.

The method of disposing of philosophy by placing it in a certain time and then saying that time is gone has been adequately dealt with by a contemporary historian. He says,

> It ascribes the birth of Aristotelianism to the fact that Aristotle was a Greek and a pagan, living in a society based on slavery, four centuries before Christ; it also explains the revival of Aristotelianism in the thirteenth century by the fact that St. Thomas Aquinas was an Italian, a Christian, and even a monk, living in a feudal society, whose political and economic structure was widely different from that of fourth-century Greece; and it accounts equally well for the Aristotelianism of J. [Jacques] Maritain, who is French, a layman, and living in the "bourgeois" society of a nineteenth-century republic. Conversely, since they were living in the same times and the same places, just as Aristotle should have held the same philosophy as Plato, so [Peter] Abelard and St. Bernard, St. Bonaventura and St. Thomas Aquinas, [René] Descartes and [Pierre] Gassendi, all these men, who flatly contradicted one another, should have said more or less the same things.

You will see at once that skepticism and presentism are related to a third ism that distorts our view of the method of education for social improvement. This is the cult of scientism, a cult to which, curiously enough, very few natural scientists belong. It is a cult composed of those who misconceive the nature or the role of science. They say that science is modern; science is tentative; science is progressive. Everything which is not science is antiquated, reactionary, or at best irrelevant. A writer in so respectable and learned a publication as the *International Journal of Ethics* has called upon us to follow science in our quest for the good life, and the fact that he is a philosopher suggests that the cult of scientism has found members in the most unlikely places. For it must be clear that though we can and should use science to achieve social improvement, we cannot follow it to this destination. The reason is that science does not tell us where to go. Men may employ it for good or evil purposes; but it is the men that have the purposes, and they do not learn them from their scientific studies.

Scientism is a disservice to science. The rise of science is the most important fact of modern life. No student should be permitted to complete his education without understanding it. Universities should and must support and encourage scientific research. From a scientific education we may expect an understanding of science. From scientific investigation we may expect scientific knowledge. We are confusing the issue and demanding what we have no right to ask if we seek to learn from science the goals of human life and of organized society.

The Dangers of Feeling Without Thought

Finally, we have the cult of anti-intellectualism, which has some oddly assorted members. They range from Hitler, who thinks with his red corpuscles, through the members of the three other cults, to men of good will, who, since they are men of good will, are at the opposite pole to Hitler, but who can give no rational justification for being there. They hold that philosophy of the heart which Auguste Comte first celebrated. Comte belonged to the cult of scientism. Therefore he could know nothing but what science told him. But he wanted social improvement. Hence he tried to make a philosophy and finally a religion out of science, and succeeded only in producing something which was no one of the three and which was, in fact, little more than sentimentalism.

Sentimentalism is an irrational desire to be helpful to one's fellow-men. It sometimes appears as an ingratiating and even a redeeming quality in those who cannot or will not think. But the sentimentalist is really a dangerous character. He distrusts the intellect, because it might show him he was wrong. He believes in the primacy of the will, and this is what makes him dangerous. You don't know what you ought to want; you don't know why you want what you want. But you do know that you want it. This easily develops into the notion that since you want it, you ought to have it. You are a man of good will, and your opponents by definition are not. Since you ought to have what you want, you should get it if you have the power; and here the journey from the man of good will to Hitler is complete.

This is indeed the position in which the members of all four cults—skepticism, presentism, scientism, and anti-intellectualism—find themselves on questions of social improvement. Since they cannot know, they must feel. We can only hope that they will feel good. But we cannot be very hopeful. Where does the good will come from? The campaign before the Austrian plebiscite [a vote by the people of an entire country to determine an issue of national importance], brought us the news that Hitler is now guided by a special revelation. Most other men of good will do not claim intimate contact with the Deity. But they are uniformly mysterious about the source of their inspiration. If it is not knowledge, and hence in this case philosophy, it must be habit and habit of the most irrational kind. A university can have nothing to do with irrational habits, except to try to moderate the bad ones and support the good ones. But if by hypothesis we cannot do this by rational means, we are forced to the conclusion that a university must be a large nursery school, tenderly preserving good habits from shock, in the hope that if they can be nursed long enough they will last through life, though without any rational foundation. In this view the boarding-school in the country would be the only proper training ground for American youth, and the University of Chicago could take no part in social improvement. In fact, it would be a subversive institution.

It hardly helps us here to say, as many anti-intellectuals do, that education must educate "the whole man." Of all the meaningless phrases in educational discussion this is the prize. Does it mean that education must do the whole job of translating the whole infant into the whole adult? Must it do what the church, the family, the state, the Y.M.C.A., and the Boy Scouts allege they are trying to do? If so, what is the place of these important or interesting organizations, and what becomes of that intellectual training which educational institutions might be able to give if they could get around to it? Are we compelled to assume that our students can learn nothing from life or that they have led no life before coming to us and lead none after they come? Moreover, what we are seeking is a guide to the emphasis that higher education must receive. Talk of the whole man seems to imply that there should be no emphasis at all. All "parts" of the man are of equal importance: his dress, his food, his health, his family, his business. Is education to emphasize them all? That would be like saying, if we were going to study the financial situation, that in studying it we should emphasize the financial situation. A flat equality among subjects, interests, and powers will hardly lead to the satisfactory development of any. Is it too much to say that if we can teach our students to lead the life of reason we shall do all that can be expected of us and do at the same time the best thing that can be done for the whole man? The task of education is to make rational animals more perfectly rational.

We see, then, that the quest for social improvement is a perpetual one. Men have always wanted not a different society, but a better one. What a better society is and how to get it has been one of the persistent problems of philosophy and one of the fundamental issues in the tradition of the Western World. Only those who recognize the important place that philosophy and the wisdom of the race must hold in education for citizenship can hope to educate men and women who can contribute to the improvement of society and who will want to do so. The cults of skepticism, presentism, scientism, and anti-intellectualism can lead us only to despair, not merely of education, but of society.

CHAPTER
F I V E

The Critics of the New Deal

Roosevelt and Ruin

Charles E. Coughlin

Reverend Charles E. (Father) Coughlin was a small-town priest who in the 1930s became one of America's most popular radio commentators. As the depression worsened, Father Coughlin turned his commentary to political and economic issues, mixing biblical rhetoric with his economic philosophy. Coughlin's attacks on big business appealed to the lower- and middle-class listeners who bore the brunt of the depression.

Soon after Franklin Delano Roosevelt was elected president of the United States, Father Coughlin gave Roosevelt his full support. This support waned, however, when Roosevelt began to reject Coughlin's proposals. For example, when Roosevelt vetoed a bill promising bonuses to World War I veterans, Coughlin told his listeners that "God hates a hypocrite."

In the following excerpt from a national radio broadcast aired on June 19, 1936, Father Coughlin, who had coined the phrase "Roosevelt or ruin," declares that because Roosevelt failed to keep his promises, Coughlin must change his words to "Roosevelt and ruin." Coughlin tells his radio audience that Roosevelt appeared like a savior, promising to rescue the American people from the greed and exploitation of big money and big business. Coughlin reveals, however, that Roosevelt failed to keep his pledge and, therefore, cannot be trusted. Despite the loss of Coughlin's support, Roosevelt defeated the Republican candidate, Alf Landon, in 1936.

Charles E. Coughlin, "Roosevelt and Ruin," radio address, June 19, 1936.

Ladies and gentlemen:
     In the Autumn of 1932, it was my privilege to address the American people on the causes of the so-called depression and upon the obvious remedies required to bring about a permanent recovery.

Those were days which witnessed a complete breakdown of the financial system under which our Western civilization had been developed. It was also evident that under this financial system there resulted a concentration of wealth and a multiplication of impoverished families. Unjust wages and unreasonable idleness were universally recognized as contradictions in an age of plenty.

To my mind it was inconceivable that irrational and needless want should exist in an age of plenty. Were there not plenty of raw materials in America? Were not our citizens and our countryside inhabited by plenty of skilled inventors, engineers, executives, workmen and farmers? At no time in the history of civilization was it possible for man to produce such an abundant supply, thanks to the benedictions of mass production machinery. At no time within the last two centuries was there such a demand on the part of our population for the thousands of good things capable of being produced in our fields and in our factories.

An Inadequate Financial System

What was the basic cause which closed factories, which created idleness, which permitted weeds to overrun our golden fields and plowshares to rust? There was and is but one answer. Some call it lack of purchasing power. Others, viewing the problem in a more philosophic light, recognize that the financial system which was able to function in an age of scarcity was totally inadequate to operate successfully in an age of plenty.

Let me explain this statement briefly: Before the nineteenth century, the ox-cart, the spade and the crude instruments of production were handicaps to the rapid creation of real wealth.

By 1932, a new era of production had come into full bloom. It was represented by the motor car, the tractor and the power lathe, which enabled the laborer to produce wealth ten times more rapidly than was possible for his ancestors. Within the short expanse of 150 years, the problem of production had been solved, due to the ingenuity of men like [Richard] Arkwright and his loom, [Robert] Fulton and his steam engine, and [Thomas] Edison and his dynamo. These and a thousand other benefactors of mankind made it possible for the teeming millions of people throughout the world to transfer speedily the raw materials into the thousand necessities and conveniences which fall under the common name of wealth.

Thus, with the advent of our scientific era, with its far-flung fields, its spacious factories, its humming motors, its thundering locomotives, its highly trained mechanics, it is inconceivable how such a thing as a so-called depression should blight the lives of an entire nation when there was a plenitude of everything surrounding us, only to be withheld from us because the so-called leaders of high finance persisted in clinging to an outworn theory of privately issued money, the medium through which wealth is distributed. . . .

A Savior Appears

Before the year 1932, very few persons fully realized the existence of this financial bondage. Millions of citizens began asking the obvious questions: "Why should the farmer be forced to follow his plow at a loss?" "Why should the citizens—at least 90 per cent of them—be imprisoned behind the cruel bars of want when, within their grasp, there are plenty of shoes, of clothing, of motor cars, of refrigerators, to which they are entitled?" At last, when the most brilliant minds amongst the industrialists, bankers and their kept politicians had failed to solve the cause of the needless depression, there appeared upon the scene of our national life a new champion of the people, Franklin Delano Roosevelt! He spoke golden words of hope. He intimated to the American people that the system of permitting a group of private citizens to create money, then to issue it to the government as if it were real money, then to exact payment from the entire nation through a system of taxation earned by real labor and service, was immoral. With the whip of his scorn he castigated these usurers who exploited the poor. With his eloquent tongue he lashed their financial system which devoured the homes of widows and orphans. No man in modern times received such plaudits from the poor as did Franklin Roosevelt when he promised to drive the money-changers from the temple—the money-changers who had clipped the coins of wages, who had manufactured spurious money, and who had brought proud America to her knees.

March 4, 1933! I shall never forget the inaugural address, which seemed to re-echo the very words employed by Christ Himself as He actually drove the money-changers from the temple. The thrill that was mine was yours. Through dim clouds of the depression, this man Roosevelt was, as it were, a new savior of his people! Oh, just a little longer shall there be needless poverty! Just another year shall there be naked backs! Just another moment shall there be dark thoughts of revolution! Never again will the chains of economic poverty bite into the hearts of simple folks, as they did in the past days of the Old Deal! Such were our hopes in the springtime of 1933. It is not pleasant for me who coined the phrase "Roosevelt *or* ruin"—a phrase fashioned upon promises—to voice such passionate words. But I am constrained to admit that "Roosevelt *and* ruin" is the order of the day, because the money-changers have not been driven from the temple.

A Failed Promise

My friends, I come before you tonight not to ask you to return to . . . the [Herbert] Hoovers, to the Old Deal exploiters, who honestly defended the dishonest system of gold standardism and rugged individualism. Their sun has set never to rise again. America has turned its back definitely upon the platitudinous platforms of "rugged individualism." These Punch and Judy Republicans, whose actions and words were dominated by the ventriloquists of Wall Street, are so blind that they do not recognize, even in this perilous hour, that their gold basis and their private coinage of money have bred more radicals than did Karl Marx or [Vladimir] Lenin. To their system or ox-cart financialism we must never return!

On the other hand, the Democratic platform is discredited before it is published. Was there not a 1932 platform? By Mr. Roosevelt and its colleagues, was it not regarded as a solemn pledge to the people? Certainly! [But] it was plowed under like the cotton, slaughtered like the pigs. . . . Therefore, the veracity of the future upstage pledges must be judged by the echoings of the golden voice of a lost leader.

Said he, when the flag of hope was proudly unfurled on March 4, 1933: "Plenty is at our doorsteps, but the generous use of it languished in the very sight of the supply. . . . Primarily, this is because the rulers of the exchange of mankind's goods have failed through their own stubbornness and their own incompetence—have admitted their failure and abdicated. Practices of the unscrupulous money-changers stand indicted in the court of public opinion, rejected by the hearts and minds of men. . . ."

These words, my friends, are not mine. These are the caustic, devastating words uttered by Franklin Delano Roosevelt on March 4, 1933, condemning Franklin Delano Roosevelt in November of 1936.

Alas! The temple still remains the private property of the money-changers. The golden key has been handed over to them for safekeeping—the key which now is fashioned in the shape of a double cross!

The New Deal Failed to Live Up to Its Promise

Alfred Emanuel Smith

Alfred Emanuel Smith began his political career in New York City and served four terms as governor of the state of New York. Smith was also the Democratic candidate for president of the United States in 1928, campaigning as the champion of urban America. Smith's Roman Catholicism, his stand against Prohibition, and his un-popularity in the rural West and South ensured his defeat to the Republican candidate, Herbert Hoover.

Although Smith supported Roosevelt in 1932, he be-came frustrated with Roosevelt's New Deal policies. Along with others who opposed the New Deal, Smith founded the "American Liberty League," which promised to "defend and uphold the Constitution" and to "foster the right to work, earn, save, and acquire property." The league supported Republican candidates for president in 1936 and 1940.

In the following address given at an American Liberty League dinner in Washington, D.C., on January 25, 1936, and broadcast on national radio, Smith speaks against the dangers of Roosevelt's New Deal. Smith reviews the planks of Roosevelt's 1932 platform and reveals how the New Deal failed to fulfill its promises. Smith also claims that the New Deal mirrors the Socialist agenda and threatens the principles of American democracy by erod-ing states' rights, interfering with the Constitution's checks and balances, and threatening individual liberty.

Alfred Emanuel Smith, address to the American Liberty League, Washington, D.C., January 25, 1936.

M r. Chairman, members and guests of the American Liberty League, and my friends listening in, as I have been told by the newspapers, from all parts of the United States: At the outset of my remarks let me make one thing perfectly clear. I am not a candidate for any nomination by any party, at any time. What is more, I do not intend even to lift my right hand to secure any nomination from any party at any time.

Further than that, I have no axe to grind. There is nothing personal in this whole performance in so far as I am concerned. I have no feeling against any man, woman or child in the United States. I am in possession of supreme happiness and comfort. I represent no group, no man, and I speak for no man or no group, but I do speak for what I believe to be the best interests of the great rank and file of the American people in which class I belong.

Now, I am here tonight also because I have a great love for the United States of America. I love it for what I know it has meant to mankind since the day of its institution. I love it because I feel that it has grown to be a great stabilizing force in world civilization. I love it, above everything else, for the opportunity that it offers to every man and every woman that desires to take advantage of it.

No man that I know of or that I probably ever read of has any more reason to love it than I have. They kept the gateway open for me. It is a matter of common knowledge throughout the country, and I do not state it boastfully, because it is well known, that, deprived by poverty in my early years of an education, that gateway showed me how it was possible to go from a newsboy on the sidewalks of New York to the Governorship of the greatest State in the Union.

Now listen. I have five children and I have ten grandchildren, and you take it from me I want that gate left open, not alone for mine—I am not selfish about it—not for mine, but for every boy and girl in the country. And in that respect I am no different from every father and mother in the United States.

Now, think it over for a minute, figure it out for yourself. It is possible for your children's success to be your success.

I remember distinctly my first inauguration as Governor of New York, and I am not sure that the young folks understood it thoroughly, but there were three people at that inauguration that did understand it: One was my mother, and the other was my sister, and the third was my wife, because they were with me in all of the early struggles.

I am here for another reason. I am here because I am a Democrat. I was born in the Democratic party and I expect to die in it. I was attached to it in my youth, because I was led to believe that no man owned it. Furthermore, that no group of men owned it, but, on the other hand, it belonged to all the plain people of the United States.

Speaking Up About the Dangers

Now, I must make a confession. It is not easy for me to stand up here tonight and talk to the American people against a Democratic administration. It is not easy; it hurts me. But I can call upon innumerable witnesses to testify to the fact that during my whole public life I put patriotism above partisanship.

And when I see danger, I see danger. That is the stop, look and listen to the fundamental principles upon which this government of ours was organized. And it is difficult for me to refrain from speaking up. What are these dangers that I see? The first is the arraignment of class against class. It has been freely predicted that if we were ever to have civil strife again in this country it would come from the appeal to the passions and prejudices that come from the demagogues who would incite one class of our people against the other.

Of course in my time I met some good and bad industrialists. I met some good and bad financiers, but I also met some good and bad laborers. This I know—that permanent prosperity is dependent upon both capital and labor alike. I also know that there can be no permanent prosperity in this country until industry is able to employ labor, and there certainly can be no permanent recovery upon any governmental theory of soak the rich or soak the poor.

Even the children in our high schools, and let it be said in the glory of our educational institutions, that even the children in our high schools know that you can't soak capital without soaking labor at the same time.

The next thing that I view as being dangerous to our national liberty's government by bureaucracy instead of what we have been taught to look to: government by law. Just let me quote something from the President's message to Congress:

"In thirty-four months we have set up new instruments of public power in the hands of the people's government, which power is wholesome and appropriate, but in the hands of political puppets of an economic autocracy, such power would provide shackles for the liberties of our people."

Now, I interpret that to mean that, if you are going to have an autocrat, take me.

But be very careful about the other fellow.

There is a complete answer to that, and it rises in the minds of the great rank and file, and that answer is just this—we will never, in this country, tolerate any law that provides shackles for our people.

We don't want any autocrats, either in or out of office. We wouldn't even take a good one.

The next thing that is apparent to me is the vast building up of new bureaus of government, draining the resources of our people, to pool and redistribute them, not by any process of law but by the whim of the bureaucratic autocracy.

Well, now, what am I here for? I am here not to find fault. Anybody can do that. I am here to make a suggestion. Now, what would I have my party do? I would have them re-establish and re-declare the principles that they put forth in that 1932 platform.

Even our Republican friends, and I know many of them—they talk to me freely, we have our little confidences among ourselves—they have all agreed that it is the most compact, the most direct and the most intelligent political platform that was ever put forth by any political party in this country.

The Republican platform was ten times as long as it. It was stuffy, it was unreadable, and in many points not understandable.

No administration in the history of the country came into power with a more simple, a more clear, or a more inescapable mandate than the party that was inaugurated on the 4th of March in 1933, and, listen, no candidate in the history of the country ever pledged himself more unequivocally to his party platform than did the President who was inaugurated on that day.

Well, here we are. Millions and millions of Democrats, just like myself, all over the country, still believe in that platform. What we want to know is, why wasn't it carried out?

And listen, there is only one man in the United States of America that can answer that question.

It won't do to pass it down to an Under-Secretary. I won't even recognize him when I hear his name. I won't know where he came from. I will be sure that he never lived down in my district.

The Democratic Platform of 1932

Now, let us wander for a little while and let us take a look at that platform and let us see what happened to it. Here is the way it started out:

"We believe that a party platform is a covenant with the people to be faithfully kept by the party when entrusted with power and that the people are entitled to know in plain words the terms of the contract to which they are asked to subscribe.

"The Democratic party solemnly promises by appropriate action to put into effect the principles, policies and reforms herein advocated and to eradicate the political methods and practices herein condemned."

My friends, these were what we called "fighting words." At the time that that platform went through the air and over the wire, the people of the United States were in the lowest possible depths of despair, and the Democratic platform looked to them like a star of hope, it looked like the rising sun in the East to the mariner on the bridge of a ship after a terrible night, but what happened to it?

First plank: "We advocate an immediate drastic reduction of governmental expenditures by abolishing useless commissions and offices, consolidating departments and bureaus, and eliminating extravagance, to accomplish a saving of not less than twenty-five per cent in the cost of the Federal Government."

Well, now, what is the fact?

No bureaus were eliminated, but on the other hand the alphabet was exhausted in the creation of new departments and—this is sad news for the taxpayer—the cost, the ordinary cost, what we refer to as "housekeeping costs" over and above all emergencies, that ordinary housekeeping cost of government is greater today than it has ever been in any time in the history of the Republic.

Another plank: "We favor maintenance of the national credit by a Federal budget annually balanced on the basis of accurate executive estimates within revenue."

Why, how can you balance a budget if you insist upon spending more money than you take in? Even the increased revenue won't go to balance the budget, because it is "hocked" before you receive it.

It is much worse than that. We borrow. We owe something. We have borrowed so that we have reached a new high peak of Federal indebtedness for all time. Well, that wouldn't annoy me so very much ordinarily.

When I was Governor of New York, they said I borrowed a lot of money. That wouldn't worry me. If it solved our problems and we were out of trouble, I would say, "All right, let it go." But the sin of it is that we have the indebtedness, and at the end of three years we are just where we started.

Unemployment and the farm problem we still have with us. Now, here is something that I want to say to the rank and file: There are three classes of people in this country, there is the poor and the rich and in between the two is what has often been referred to as the great backbone of America, that is the plain fellow, that is the fellow that makes from $100 a month up to the man that draws down five or six thousand dollars a year.

Now, there is that great big army. Forget the rich; they can't pay this debt; if you took everything they got away from them you could not pay it, there are not enough of them.

Furthermore, they ain't got enough. Now, there's no use of talking about the poor. They will never pay it, because they got nothing. This debt is going to be paid by that great big middle-class that we refer to as the backbone and the rank and file, and the sin of it is, they ain't going to know that they're paying it.

It is going to come to them in the form of indirect taxation. It will come in the cost of living, in the cost of clothing, in the cost of every activity they enter into, and because it isn't a direct tax, they won't think they are paying it, but take it from me, they are going to pay it.

Another point: "We advocate the extension of Federal credit to the States to provide for unemployment relief when the diminishing resources of the State render it impossible to provide for them."

That is pretty plain.

That was a recognition in the national convention of the rights of the States. But what happened? The Federal Government took over most of the relief problems, some of them useful and most of them useless. They started out to prime the pump for industry in order to absorb the ranks of the unemployed, and at the end of three years their affirmative policy is absolutely nothing but the negative policy of the administration that preceded it.

We favor unemployment and old age insurance under State laws. Now, let me make myself perfectly clear so that no demagogue or no crack pot in the next week or so will be able to say anything about my attitude on this kind of legislation. I am in favor of it, and I take my hat off to no man in the United States on the question of legislation beneficial to the poor, the weak, the sick or the afflicted, men, women and children.

Because when I started out a quarter of a century ago, when I had very few followers in my State, during that period I advocated, fought for and introduced, as a legislator, and finally as Governor, for eight long years, and signed more progressive legislation in the interest of men, women and children than any man in the State of New York. And the sin of this whole thing, and the part of it that worries me and gives me concern is, that this haphazard legislation is never going to accomplish the purpose for which it was designed. And bear this in mind—follow the platform—under State law."

A Record of Failed Promises

Here is another one: "We promise the enactment of every constitutional measure that will aid the farmers to receive for their basic farm commodities prices in excess of cost."

Well, what is the use of talking about that? "We promise

every constitutional measure." The Supreme Court disposed of that within the last couple of weeks. And, according to the papers the other day, some brilliant individual has conceived the idea of how to get around the Constitution. We are going to have forty-eight AAA's [Agricultural Adjustment Acts], one for each State.

The day that the United States Supreme Court decided the case I left my office to attend a board of trustees meeting. I got in a taxicab to go downtown. The driver was reading the extra, "Supreme Court Declares AAA Unconstitutional."

We rode along for a few minutes and then we got caught at a red light. The taxi fellow turned around and said: "Governor, ain't there any lawyers in Congress any more?"

Just then the lights changed. I was afraid to answer him for fear I might disconcert him but I was all ready to say: "Yes, son, but they don't function."

We got another plank! "We advocate strengthening and impartial enforcement of the anti-trust laws." What happened? The NRA [National Recovery Administration] just put a gas bag on the anti-trust laws and put them fast asleep.

And nobody said anything about it. I don't know whether they are good or whether they are bad, but I know that they didn't work.

Another one: "We promise the removal of government from all fields of private enterprise, except where necessary to develop public works and national resources in the common interest."

NRA! A vast octopus set up by government that wound its arms around all the business of the country, paralyzed big business and choked little business to death.

Did you read in the papers a short time ago where somebody said that business was going to get a breathing spell? What is the meaning of that? And where did that expression arise? I will tell you where it comes from.

It comes from the prize ring. When the aggressor is punching the head off the other fellow, he suddenly takes compassion on him and gives him a breathing spell before he delivers the knockout wallop.

Here is another one: "We condemn the open and covert resistance of administrative officials to every effort made by

Congressional committees to curtail the extravagance and expenses of government and improvident subsidies rendered to private interests."

Now, just between ourselves, do you know any administrative officer that ever tried to stop Congress from appropriating money? Do you think there has been any desire on the part of Congress to curtail appropriations?

Why, not at all. The fact is, that Congress is throwing them left and right, don't even tell what they are for.

And the truth is that every administrative officer sought to get all he possibly could, to expand the activities of his own office, and throw the money of the people right and left.

As to the subsidy—never at any time in the history of this or any other country were there so many subsidies granted to private groups and on such a large scale. The fact of the matter is that most of the cases pending before the United States Supreme Court revolve around the point of whether or not it is proper for Congress to tax all the people to pay subsidies to a particular group.

Here is another one: "We condemn the extravagance of the Farm Board, its disastrous action which made the government a speculator in farm products, and the unsound policy of restricting agricultural products to the demands of domestic markets."

Listen, and I will let you in on something. This has not leaked out, so kind of keep it to yourself until you get the news.

On the first of February we are going to own 4,500,000 bales of cotton. The cost is $270,000,000.

And we have been such brilliant speculators that we are paying thirteen cents a pound for it when you add storage and carrying charges, and it can be bought in any one of the ten cotton markets of the South today for $11.50. Some speculators!

What about the restriction of our agricultural products and the demands of the domestic market? Why, the fact about that is that we shut out entirely the foreign market, and by plowing under corn and wheat and the destruction of foodstuffs, food from foreign countries has been pouring into our American markets, food that should have been purchased by us from our own farmers.

In other words, while some of the countries of the Old

World were attempting to drive the wolf of hunger from the doormat, the United States of America flew in the face of God's bounty and destroyed its own foodstuffs. There can be no question about that.

Now, I could go on indefinitely with some of the other planks. They are unimportant and the radio time will not permit it. But just let me sum up this way: regulation of the Stock Exchange and the repeal of the Eighteenth Amendment, plus one or two minor provisions of the platform that in no way touched the daily life of our people have been carried out, but the balance of the platform was thrown in the waste-basket. About that there can be no question.

The New Deal Parallels the Socialist Platform

And let us see how it was carried out. Make a test for yourself.

Just get the platform of the Democratic party and get the platform of the Socialist party and lay them down on your dining-room table, side by side, and get a heavy lead pencil and scratch out the word "Democratic" and scratch out the word "Socialist" and let the two platforms lay there, and then study the record of the present administration up to date.

After you have done that, make your mind up to pick up the platform that more nearly squares with the record, and you will have your hand on the Socialist platform; you would not dare touch the Democratic platform.

And incidentally, let me say that it is not the first time in recorded history that a group of men have stolen the livery of the church to do the work of the devil.

If you study this whole situation you will find that is at the bottom of all our troubles. This country was organized on the principles of a representative democracy, and you can't mix socialism or communism with that. They are like oil and water. They are just like oil and water, they refuse to mix.

Incidentally, let me say to you that is the reason why the United States Supreme Court is working overtime, throwing the alphabet out of the window, three letters at a time.

I am going to let you in on something else. How do you suppose all this happened? The young brain trusters caught the

Socialists in swimming and they ran away with their clothes.

Now, it is all right with me, it is all right with me, if they want to disguise themselves as Karl Marx or [Vladimir] Lenin or any of the rest of that bunch, but I won't stand for their allowing them to march under the banner of [Andrew] Jackson or [Grover] Cleveland.

Now, what is worrying me is: Where does that leave us millions of Democrats? My mind is all fixed upon the convention in June in Philadelphia. The committee on resolutions is about to report. The preamble to the platform is:

"We, the representatives of the Democratic party, in convention assembled, heartily endorse the Democratic administration."

What happened to the recital of [Thomas] Jefferson and Jackson and Cleveland when that resolution was read out? Why, for us it is a washout. There is only one of two things we can do, we can either take on the mantle of hypocrisy or we can take a walk, and we will probably do the latter.

Now, leave the platform alone for a little while. What about this attack that has been made upon the fundamental institutions of this country, who threatens them, and did we have any warning of this threat? Why, you don't have to study party platforms, you don't have to read books, you don't have to listen to professors of economics. You will find the whole thing incorporated in the greatest declaration of political principle that ever came from the hand of man—the Declaration of Independence and the Constitution of the United States.

Always have in your mind that the Constitution and the first ten amendments were drafted by refugees and by sons of refugees, by men with bitter memories of European oppression and hardship, by men who brought to this country, and handed down to their descendants an abiding fear of arbitrary, centralized government and autocracy and—listen, all the bitterness and all the hatred of the Old World was distilled, in our Constitution, into the purest democracy that the world has ever known.

There are just three principles and in the interest of brevity I will read them. I can read them quicker than I can talk them.

First, a Federal Government strictly limited in its powers, with all other powers except those expressly mentioned reserved to the States and to the people, so as to insure State's rights, guarantee home rule and preserve freedom of individual initiative and local control.

That is simple enough. The difference between the State Constitution and the Federal Constitution is that in the State you can do anything you want to do provided it is not prohibited by the Constitution, but in the Federal Government, according to that document, you can do only that which that Constitution tells you that you can do.

What is the trouble? Congress has overstepped its power, it has gone beyond that constitutional limitation, and it has enacted laws that not only violate that, but violate the home rule and the State's rights principle. And who says that?

Did I say it? Not at all. That was said by the United States Supreme Court in the last ten or twelve days.

Second, the government with three independent branches, Congress to make the laws, the Executives to execute them, the Supreme Court, and so forth, and you all know that.

In the name of heaven, where is the independence of Congress? Why, they just laid right down. They are flatter on the Congressional floor than the rug under this table here.

They centered all their powers in the Executives, and that is the reason why you read in the newspapers reference to Congress as the rubber-stamp Congress.

We all know that the most important bills were drafted by the brain trusters and sent over to Congress and passed by Congress without consideration, without debate, and, without meaning any offense at all to my Democratic brethren in Congress, I think I can safely say without 90 percent of them knowing what was in the bills, what was the meaning of the list that came over, and beside certain items was "must."

Speaking for the rank and file of the American people, we don't want any Executive to tell Congress what it must do. We don't want any Congress to tell the Executive what he must do.

We don't want Congress or the Executive, jointly or severally, to tell the United States Supreme Court what it must do.

On the other hand, we don't want the United States

Supreme Court to tell either of them what they must do.
What we want, and what we insist upon, and what we are
going to have, is the absolute preservation of this balance of
power which is the keystone upon which the whole theory of
democratic government has got to rest, and when you rattle
it you rattle the whole structure.

Of course, when our forefathers wrote the Constitution,
it couldn't be possible that they had in their minds that that
was going to be all right for all time to come, so they said,
"No, we will provide a manner and method of amending,"
and that is set forth in the document itself. And during our
national life we amended it many times.

We amended it once by mistake, and we corrected it.

And what did we do? We took the amendment out. Fine!
That is the way we ought to do it. By recourse to the people.

But we don't want an administration that takes a shot at
it in the dark and that ducks away from it and dodges away
from it and tries to put something over in contradiction of it
upon any theory that there is going to be a great public
power in favor of it and it is possible that the United States
Supreme Court may be intimidated into a friendly opinion
with respect to it.

But I found all during my public life that Almighty God
built this country and He did not give us that kind of a
Supreme Court.

Now, this is pretty tough for me to have to go after my
own party this way, but I submit that there is a limit to blind
loyalty.

As a young man in the Democratic party I witnessed the
rise and fall of [William Jennings] Bryan and Bryanism, and
in the memory of Bryan, what he did to our party, I know
how long it took to build it after he got finished with it. But
let me say this, for the everlasting memory of Bryan and the
men that followed him, that they had the energy and the
courage and the honesty to put into the platform just what
their leaders told them.

They put the American people in the position of making an
intelligent choice when they went to the polls. The fact of this
whole thing is, I speak now not only of the Executive but of
the Legislature at the same time—that they promised one set

of things. They repudiated that promise, and they launched off on a program of action totally different.

Well, in twenty-five years of experience I have known both parties to fail to carry out some of the planks of their platform, but this is the first time that I have known a party, upon such a huge scale, not only not to carry out the planks, but to do directly the opposite thing to what they promised.

Suggestions for the Democratic Party

Now, suggestions—and I make these as a Democrat, acting for the success of my party, and I make them in good faith. Here are my suggestions:

Number 1—I suggest for the members of my party on Capitol Hill here in Washington that they take their minds off the Tuesday that follows the first Monday in November.

Just take your mind off it to the end that you may do the right thing and not the expedient thing.

Yes, I suggest to them that they dig up the 1932 platform from the grave that they buried it in and read it over and study it, read life into it and follow it in legislative and executive action to the end that they make good their promises to the American people when they put forth that platform and the candidate that stood upon it 100 percent—in short, make good.

Third, I would suggest that they stop compromising with the fundamental principles laid down by Jackson and Jefferson and Cleveland.

Fourth, stop attacking all the forms of the structure of our government without recourse to the people themselves, as provided in their own Constitution which really belongs to the people, and it does not belong to any administration.

Next, I suggest that they read their oath of office to support the Constitution of the United States and I ask them to remember that they took that oath with their hands on the Holy Bible, thereby calling upon God Almighty himself to witness their solemn promise. It is bad enough to disappoint us.

Sixth, I suggest that from this moment on they resolve to make the Constitution again the Civil Bible of the United States and to pay it the same civil respect and reverence that they would religiously pay the Holy Scripture, and I ask them to read from the Holy Scripture the paragraph of the prodigal son, and to follow his example, "Stop, stop wasting your substance in a foreign land and come back to your father's house."

Now, in conclusion, let me give this solemn warning: There can be only one capital, Washington or Moscow.

There can be only one atmosphere of government, the clear, pure, fresh air of free America, or the foul breath of communistic Russia. There can be only one flag, the Stars and Stripes, or the flag of the godless Union of the Soviets.

There can be only one national anthem, "The Star-Spangled Banner" or the "Internationale."

There can be only one victor. If the Constitution wins, we win.

But if the Constitution—stop, stop there—the Constitution can't lose.

The fact is, it has already won, but the news has not reached certain ears.

The New Deal Erodes States' Rights

Eugene Talmadge

Although President Franklin D. Roosevelt and Eugene Talmadge were both Democrats, Talmadge, four-time governor of Georgia, represented the conservative state politics of the South, which had little in common with the expansionist policies of Roosevelt's administration. Talmadge originally supported Roosevelt, calling for decreased taxes and federal programs to support the southern economy. However, when federal programs began to dictate local policy—telling farmers what crops they could plant and manufacturers how much to pay their labor—Talmadge, like many other Democrats, began to attack Roosevelt's administration.

Talmadge was famous for his political rallies where attendees were provided food, pamphlets, and campaign buttons. Talmadge would speak from a stand festooned with flags, and would appeal to the experiences, values, and prejudices of his listeners. Talmadge did not prepare his speeches and often enlisted support from his audience, asking questions to which his audience would shout responses such as "Tell it like it is!"

In January 1936, several wealthy supporters sponsored a "grass roots" convention in Macon, Georgia, to nominate Talmadge as a Democratic presidential candidate. On January 29, 1936, Talmadge delivered the following speech attacking Roosevelt's New Deal programs. Talmadge reminds his listeners that the South has always defended states' rights. The New Deal programs of the Roosevelt administration, however, have been eroding

Eugene Talmadge, address to "grass roots" convention, Macon, Georgia, January 29, 1936.

state sovereignty, keeping the nation in poverty as a result
of the administration's shameful economic policy of
scarcity. Talmadge encourages southern Democrats to demand a return to the Democratic principles of Thomas
Jefferson, who warned America of the dangers of autocrats, and Andrew Jackson who, unlike Roosevelt, kept
his promise to the nation.

The south has been the champion and the defender of
democratic principles for three-quarters of a century.
The south has fought for states' rights. That great conflict is over. We are back to the Union, and back to stay. The
south wishes to share her part of the burdens and responsibilities of the national government. States' rights are in the balance today more than they were in the days of 1861. At that
time, states' rights were obliterated by humanitarian pleas for
the freedom of slaves. Today, in every capital of the various
states, and in every county site in America, the federal government is working consistently to tear down states' rights.

If the present program is continued for four more years,
the lines between the states will be only a shadow on paper,
and the government of the separate states will be subservient
to the will of a central power at Washington. This time, there
is nothing to becloud the issues of sovereignty of states and
local self-government. Our brothers in the east, and north,
and west are with us to see that local self-government and the
sovereignty of our separate states is not obliterated by the
whims of bureaucrats.

A Shameful Administration

Every true democrat hangs his head in shame when he realizes that under a democratic administration are boards, and
boards, and boards—and that the President in Washington
[Franklin D. Roosevelt] has had enacted laws where they
could tell the manufacturers, store keepers, hotels and shops
what to pay their labor, and how many hours they could
work. And the present administration crowned this challenge

to states' rights with the NIRA [National Industrial Recovery Act], taking for its emblem a blue eagle. The originator of the thought must have been inspired, because during the reign of the NIRA, the American eagle (emblem of our great country) was certainly blue and sad. But let's not say any more about the NIRA. It is gone. And nine months after the supreme court said that it was gone, the President said so. He then announced that he was stopping the pay of thousands of workers who were being paid millions of dollars per month out of the taxpayers' money to carry on an organization that the supreme court had ruled unconstitutional.

Again every true democrat hangs his head in shame, when he realizes that under the name of a democratic administration, boards and bureaus, and the President himself, say [sic] that the way to bring back prosperity in this country is through scarcity—have less to eat, and less to wear. To carry out this crazy, infamous plan, they ordered millions of hogs and cattle killed, and thrown into the rivers or buried. Millions more of little sucking pigs were shipped off to Chicago. On top of this, they paid a premium to get to cut a good brood sow's throat. It took a little time for this travesty but when they struck the sheep and goats, they drove them on top of the mountains, forcing them to jump off the cliffs and kill themselves in the valleys below. And when the starving people went there to retrieve some of these carcasses that were not too badly mangled by the rocks, the trained welfare workers ran them off, leaving them as food only for the coyotes and wolves. They burned up wheat and oats, and plowed under cotton here in the south.

Yet, in Washington, with their faces wreathed in smiles, they were telling the people that they were bringing back "the abundant life." And something else happened too, while all this was going on! What next do we see? Importation in greater numbers than ever before of these same products that had been destroyed here in America. And they are announcing that they want to keep it up!

When the supreme court again saved America by saying that the AAA [Agricultural Adjustment Act] was unconstitutional, announcements came from Washington that [Rexford G.] Tugwell, [Felix] Frankfurter, [Henry] Wallace and even the President himself were studying and looking for plans to devise a law that would get around the supreme court, and continue their policy of scarcity here in America. They do all of this under the name of a democratic administration.

Challenging State Sovereignty

What else do they do? They have cabinet officers who try to intimidate governors, and legislatures to pass their New Deal legislation in order to centralize government in Washington.

I am sad to say that some of the governors in these United States have "goose-stepped" into line and saddled on their states and counties taxes that it will take a century to pay, giving over the freedom and the sovereignty of their states to boards and bureaucrats in Washington. Georgia did not "goose-step" on the New Deal bills which they sent down to Atlanta to me to be crammed through the legislature, providing for thousands of federal jobs in the state of Georgia at the expense of the state. And when the Governor of Georgia [Talmadge] did not "goose-step" he was labeled by a member of the cabinet as "his chain gang excellency, whose word is no good."

The only one of the New Deal bills that passed was one to defraud the bounties of the state out of the highway scrip, where they had a bonded indebtedness for roads. Secretary [of the Interior Harold L.] Ickes had accepted these highway certificates, contrary to law, and wanted to make the Governor of Georgia a party to his illegal contract.

This explains the wrath of Ickes when he tries to make the people of America believe that the word of the Governor of Georgia is not good. I hope that he is listening in at this talk, as I want to tell him something now. The people of Georgia can answer this for him, and the people of the United States are going to answer it in November of this year by driving him and all of his cohorts from Washington, and never allowing them to return.

Trying to help the farmer! Telling him what to plant on his land, and how little, and then telling him that taxing it over 50 per cent of its worth will help him! And those who were hired and given jobs with the government pretend to believe it. Before their crazy dream of "prosperity from scarcity" will ever work in this world, they will have to invent some ointment to take the place of sweat.

Returning to Democratic Principles

The democrats of the south owe it to the nation to rally to the principles of Thomas Jefferson, the founder of this party. You owe it to the north, and the east and the west to help in this fight to see that no communist or socialist steals the democratic nomination, and mocks you with smiles and jeers by telling you that the south is always solidly democratic. Yes, the south is democratic, true to the faith and true to the principles of Thomas Jefferson: "Sovereignty of states' rights"; "The least governed are the best governed"; "Local self-government." The south is going to remain true to these fundamentals of democracy.

What is the fight for the democratic party in 1936? What is the fight for all true Americans in 1936? Here it is: Shall we cling to our present form of government, or abolish it? Shall we barter away Americanism for communism?

Shall we continue to borrow and spend, or settle down and settle up? Shall we substitute lunacy for sanity? Shall we convert democrats into bureaucrats? Shall we share our wealth through charity, or lose it through taxation? Shall we replace impartial Uncle Sam with old Mother Hubbard playing favorites? Shall we remain idle and import food, or work and produce it? Shall we starve the litter of 12 to feed the thirteenth pig, or give them all a break? Shall we pamper or punish enemies without gates? Shall we march under the Stars and Stripes, or under a crazy quilt?

You Americans, good and true, cannot be bought and bribed. In self-defense, you have had to take parity checks, bicycles, skates, rat traps or any other thing that Washington thought they could buy your souls with. Washington has not been paying for these things. The government is not paying for them. The government never pays for anything. It collects the money from the people—and has made every man, woman and child in America a taxpayer a thousand-fold more than they ever dreamed.

The supreme court has come to our rescue. Let's hold up their hands. Let's don't allow a bunch of communists to have four more years to appoint the successors to such stalwart men as Chief Justice Hughes and Associate Justices Butler, McReynolds, Sutherland and Van Devanter. If the New Dealers can pick their own supreme court, the wheels of our democracy would catch fire and burn down our freedom.

The New Dealers have tried by billions of dollars to hold back a natural recovery due this country. They are determined that the bonus checks will be paid in June, so that there will be a flush of money to go on through until election time in November. But the play is too plain. No such joker can come from under the table and fool the soldiers of America who defended this country, and ask only for the payment of an acknowledged debt.

What else is the job of democrats and all other true Americans this year? Rewrite the platform of 1932! Nominate men on this platform whose word is so good that the best test of it is to have the New Dealers call him a "liar." Then America will know that his word is good. Cut taxes! Stop nine-tenths of the federal activities in America! Stop all competition of the government with private industry! Cut down the expense of the federal government by tearing down seven-eighths of the buildings in Washington, and cover the grounds with beautiful parks! Pay up the national debt!

Go back to the doctrine (not in a $50 a plate mockery celebration) of the stalwart man, Andrew Jackson, who celebrated the victory of the Battle of New Orleans by announcing to America that within one year he had kept his platform pledge, and paid up all the debts of America. Go back to the doctrine of George Washington and Thomas Jefferson, who warned us that autocrats would rise up in the name of emergency to tear down our form of government. And that sturdy soldier, George Washington, said that whenever this happens, to rise up and smite them. Nineteen hundred and thirty-six will go down in history equal in importance with July 4, 1776.

> How sure the bolt that Justice wings;
> How weak the arm a traitor brings;
> How mighty they, who steadfast stand
> For freedom's flag, and freedom's land.

Socialism, Not the New Deal, Will Restore Prosperity

Norman Mattoon Thomas

Considered one of the foremost political speakers of his time, Norman Mattoon Thomas was the Socialist Party candidate for president of the United States between 1928 and 1948. Although he severed his ties with the traditional Marxists, he remained one of the party's most popular spokesmen for many years. Thomas, a Presbyterian minister, was an outspoken pacifist and one of the founders of the American Civil Liberties Union.

Thomas criticized Roosevelt's New Deal on the basis that it stressed the solution to economic problems while neglecting social and moral issues. In the following nationwide radio address, delivered on February 2, 1936, Thomas rejects Alfred E. Smith's claim that Roosevelt's New Deal mirrors the Socialist platform of 1932. For example, Thomas argues that Socialists would not take over and restore banks only to return them to the bankers. Thomas claims that the New Deal is not socialism, but State capitalism, a system in which the government regulates production while maintaining the profit system, private ownership, and the unfair division of income. State capitalism does not protect the common good, says Thomas, but actually resembles fascism. Socialism, on the other hand, supports true democracy, Thomas maintains, because Socialists do not want to eliminate private property but rather to distribute property so that no one will go without.

Norman Mattoon Thomas, "Is the New Deal Socialism?" radio address, February 2, 1936.

T
he air rings, the newspapers are filled with the politics
of bedlam. There are still around 10,000,000 unemployed in the United States. Re-employment lags behind the increase of production, and the increase of money
wages in industry lags behind both. The burden of debt piles
higher and higher. The world, and America with it, drifts toward new war of inconceivable horror—war from which we
shall not be delivered by spending out of our poverty more
than a billion dollars a year on naval and military prepara-
tions without so much as squarely facing the issue: what are
we protecting and how shall we protect it?

A Shouting Match

In this situation the leaders of our two major political parties
have begun speaking, or rather shouting. And what do they
say? First, President Roosevelt makes a fighting speech to
Congress and the nation defending the record he has made,
but proposing no new program. Scarcely has he finished his
speech when the AAA [Agricultural Adjustment Act] decision of the Supreme Court and the enactment of the bonus
legislation by Congress compel him to seek new laws and
new taxes.

Then Mr. Roosevelt's one-time dearest political friend and
sponsor, Alfred E. Smith, rushes to the fray. This erstwhile
man of the people chooses a dinner of the Liberty League at
which to proclaim the religion of Constitution worship, favorable incidental mention of the Holy Bible, Washington as
the nation's capital and the Stars and Stripes forever.

It was attended, the newspapers tell us, by twelve
du Ponts—twelve apostles, not of liberty but of big business
and the profits of war and preparation for war. Indeed, the
record of Mr. Smith's new friends shows that that organization is as much entitled to the name Liberty League as was
the disease commonly known as German measles to be called
liberty measles in the hysteria of war.

Mr. Smith was promptly answered in a speech read, if not
written, by Senator [Joseph Taylor] Robinson, who is the
close political and personal friend of the utility magnate,
Harvey Crouch, and the protector of the plantation system

which in his own State is now answering the demands of the exploited sharecroppers by wholesale evictions and organized terror. On this subject Senator Robinson and other defenders of the New Deal preserve a profound silence.

Then the Governor of Georgia, [Eugene Talmadge], jumped into the fray along with an oil baron and Huey Long's share-the-wealth clergyman [Gerald L.K. Smith] to exploit race and sectional prejudice in the name of States' rights. These all are Democrats.

Meanwhile the Republicans who defeated Alfred E. Smith in 1928 rise to applaud him. Ex-President [Herbert] Hoover, rejuvenated by the skillful services of a new ghost writer, denounces Mr. Roosevelt's administration and proposes a plan of farm relief quite similar to Roosevelt's substitute for AAA.

Between him and the States' rights Senator [William E.] Borah, who still believes that the country can be saved by the simple device of trying to smash monopoly, there is as deep a gulf fixed as there is in the Democratic party. Alf Landon floats somewhere in that gulf.

Yet basically beneath all the alarms and confusion these worthy warriors happy and unhappy, are, acting upon a common assumption—an assumption which is dangerously false. All of them are assuming the durability of the profit system, the security of a capitalist nationalist system in which our highest loyalties are to the principle of private profit and to the political power of an absolute jingoistic nationalist State. They assume that prosperity is coming back again to stay for a while.

Mr. Roosevelt and his followers assume that prosperity is coming back because of the New Deal. Al Smith and the rest of Roosevelt's assorted critics assume that it is in spite of the New Deal and perhaps because of the Supreme Court Mr. Hoover plaintively protests that the catastrophic depression of January–February, 1933, was due merely to the shudders of the body politic anticipating the economic horrors of the New Deal.

All of these leaders or would-be leaders out of our wilderness, however they may abuse one another, however loosely they may fling around the charge of socialism or communism—the two are not the same—still accept the basic institutions and loyalties of the present system. A true Socialist is resolved to replace that system.

As a Socialist, I view the Smith-Roosevelt controversy with complete impartiality. I am little concerned to point out the inconsistencies in Al Smith's record, or to remind him that in 1924 and 1928, when I happened to be the Socialist candidate for high office against him, more than one of his close political friends came to me to urge me as a Socialist not to attack him too severely since he really stood for so many of the things that Socialists and other progressive workers wanted.

I am entirely willing to grant that Mr. Roosevelt did not carry out the Democratic platform of 1932. Could Mr. Smith have done it? As for myself, I much prefer the company in which Mr. Smith put me in his Liberty League speech to the company in which he put himself at that dinner.

The New Deal Is Not Socialism

But I am concerned to point out how false is the charge that Roosevelt and the New Deal represent socialism. What is at stake is not prestige or sentimental devotion to a particular name. What is at stake is a clear understanding of the issues on which the peace and prosperity of generations—perhaps of centuries—depend. A nation which misunderstands socialism as completely as Al Smith misunderstands it is a nation which weakens its defense against the coming of war and fascism.

But, some of you will say, isn't it true, as Alfred E. Smith and a host of others before him have charged, that Roosevelt carried out most of the demands of the Socialist platform?

This charge is by no means peculiar to Mr. Smith. I am told that a Republican speaker alleged that Norman Thomas rather than Franklin D. Roosevelt has been President of the United States. I deny the allegation and defy the allegator and I suspect I have Mr. Roosevelt's support in this denial. Matthew Woll, leader of the forces of reaction in the American Federation of Labor, is among the latest to make the same sort of charge.

Emphatically, Mr. Roosevelt did not carry out the Socialist

platform, unless he carried it out on a stretcher. What is true is that when Mr. Roosevelt took office he had to act vigorously.

He looked at the Democratic platform and he found no line on which he could act. It was all very well to pledge support to sound money, but there wasn't any money. Mr. Roosevelt gave a hasty glance at the Republican platform, or perhaps he merely contented himself by noting its musty smell. Then, perhaps, he did look at the Socialist platform. He needed ideas and there was nowhere else to look.

We had demanded Federal relief for unemployment. Hence any attempts Mr. Roosevelt made at Federal relief could perhaps be called by his enemies an imitation of the Socialist platform. It was an extraordinarily poor imitation. We demanded Federal unemployment insurance. Hence any attempt to get Federal security legislation could be regarded as an imitation of the Socialist platform. It was an amazingly bad imitation.

If we were in swimming and if Mr. Roosevelt's brain trust stole our clothes, it's a pity they didn't steal more of them and put them on more carefully. It would have been a more decent performance.

As a matter of fact, the American people on March 4, 1933, weren't in swimming. They were all caught in a blizzard. Mr. Hoover had us sitting still waiting for death or divine deliverance from around the corner, or a miraculous clearing of the storm. Mr. Roosevelt started us running. To be sure, we ran nowhere in particular, but we ran hard enough to keep the blood circulating and so did not perish from freezing. Under his program we accomplished the extraordinary feat of running in several directions at once. And that's not socialism.

Indeed, at various times Mr. Roosevelt has taken particular and rather unnecessary pains to explain that he was not a Socialist, that he was trying to support the profit system, which by the way, he defined incorrectly. In his last message to Congress his attack was not upon the profit system but on the sins of big business.

His slogan was not the Socialist cry: "Workers of the world, workers with hand and brain, in town and country, unite!" His cry was, "Workers and small stockholders unite, clean up Wall

Street." That cry is at least as old as Andrew Jackson.

What Mr. Roosevelt and his brain trust and practical political advisers did to such of the Socialist immediate demands as he copied at all merely illustrates the principle that if you want a child brought up right you had better leave the child with his parents and not farm him out to strangers. Time fails me to illustrate this point by a detailed examination of the Roosevelt emergency legislation.

Comparing Roosevelt's Policies to Socialism

Some of it was good reformism, but there is nothing Socialist about trying to regulate or reform Wall Street. Socialism wants to abolish the system of which Wall Street is an appropriate expression. There is nothing Socialist about trying to break up great holding companies. We Socialists would prefer to acquire holding companies in order to socialize the utilities now subject to them.

There was no socialism at all about taking over all the banks which fell in Uncle Sam's lap, putting them on their feet again, and turning them back to the bankers to see if they can bring them once more to ruin. There was no socialism at all about putting in a Coordinator to see if he could make the bankrupt railroad systems profitable so they would be more expensive for the government to acquire as sooner or later the government, even a Republican party government, under capitalism must.

Mr. Roosevelt torpedoed the London Economic Conference; he went blindly rushing in to a big army and navy program; he maintained, as he still maintains, an Ambassador in Cuba who, as the agent of American financial interests, supports the brutal reaction in Cuba. While professing friendship for China, he blithely supported a silver purchase policy of no meaning for America except the enrichment of silver mine owners which nearly ruined the Chinese Government in the face of Japanese imperialism. These things which Al Smith or Alf Landon might also have done are anything but Socialist.

Mr. Smith presumably feels that the President's Security Bill, so-called, was socialism. Let us see. We Socialists have long advocated unemployment insurance or unemployment indemnity by which honest men who cannot find work are indemnified by a society so brutal or so stupid that it denies them the opportunity to work. This insurance or indemnification should be on a prearranged basis which will take account of the size of the family. It should be Federal because only the national government can act uniformly, consistently and effectively.

What did Mr. Roosevelt give us? In the name of security, he gave us a bill where in order to get security the unemployed workers will first have to get a job, then lose a job. He will have to be sure that he gets the job and loses the job in a State which has an unemployment insurance law.

He will then have to be sure that the State which has the law will have the funds and the zeal to get the money to fulfill the terms of the law. This will largely depend upon whether it proves to be practical and constitutional for the Federal Government to collect a sufficient tax on payrolls so that 90 percent of it when rebated to employers to turn over to the State officers will be sufficient to give some kind of security to those who are unemployed!

The whole proceeding is so complicated, the danger of forty-eight competing State laws—competing, by the way, for minimum, not for maximum benefits—is so dangerous that the President's s bill can justly be called an in-Security bill.

If Mr. Smith means that the program of public works either under PWA [Public Works Administration] or WPA [Works Progress Administration] is Socialist, again he is mistaken. We do not tolerate the standards of pay set on much WPA work—$19 a month, for instance, in some States in the South. We do insist not upon talk but upon action to rehouse the third of America which lives in houses unfit for human habitation, which is possible given the present state of the mechanic arts in a nation of builders.

The administration, having spent billions of words, not dollars, on housing with little result, is now turning the job over to private mortgage companies. Would not Al Smith or Alf Landon do the same?

The one outstanding act of the administration that Socialists applaud is, of course, the Tennessee Valley Authority.

That of itself is not socialism. No single measure of the sort can be socialism by itself. But it is Socialist to the extent that it substitutes production for use for production for profit. However, it is an impossible task to correlate satisfactorily this type of production with the economic activities of a region still governed by the profit system.

It is this that I had in mind when in an extemporaneous speech I made the statement, so often misquoted or misinterpreted, to the effect that TVA had many merits, but that there was danger that it would be like a beautiful flower planted in a garden of weeds with great corporations watering the weeds.

But even if Mr. Roosevelt and the New Deal had far more closely approximated Socialist immediate demands in their legislation, they would not have been Socialists, not unless Mr. Smith is willing to argue that every reform, every attempt to curb rampant and arrogant capitalism, every attempt to do for the farmers something like what the tariff has done for business interests, is socialism.

Not only is it not socialism, but in large degree this State capitalism, this use of bread and circuses to keep the people quiet, is so much a necessary development of a dying social order that neither Mr. Smith nor Mr. Hoover in office in 1937 could substantially change the present picture or bring back the days of Andrew Jackson, Grover Cleveland or Calvin Coolidge.

The New Deal Is State Capitalism

What Roosevelt has given us, and what the Republicans cannot and will not substantially change, is not the socialism of the co-operative commonwealth. It is a State capitalism which the Fascist demagogues of Europe have used when they came to power. The thing, Mr. Smith, that you ought to fear is not that the party of [Thomas] Jefferson and Jackson is marching in step with Socialists toward a Socialist goal; it is that, unwittingly, it may be marching in step with Fascists toward a Fascist goal.

It is not Moscow as a rival to Washington that you should fear, but Berlin.

I do not mean that Mr. Roosevelt himself is a Fascist or

likely to become a Fascist. I credit him with as liberal intentions as capitalism and his Democratic colleagues of the South permit. I call attention to the solemn fact that in spite of his circumspect liberalism, repression, the denial of civil liberty, a Fascist kind of military law, stark terrorism have been increasing under Democratic Governors for the most part—in Indiana, Florida, Georgia, Alabama, Arkansas and, of course, in California, where Mr. Roosevelt did not even come to the aid of an ex-Socialist, Upton Sinclair, against the candidate of the reactionaries.

I repeat that what Mr. Roosevelt has given us is State capitalism; that is to say, a system under which the State steps in to regulate and in many cases to own, not for the purpose of establishing production for use but rather for the purpose of maintaining in so far as may be possible the profit system with its immense rewards of private ownership and its grossly unfair division of the national income.

Today Mr. Roosevelt does not want fascism; Mr. Hoover does not want fascism; not even Mr. Smith and his friends of the Liberty League want fascism. The last-named gentlemen want an impossible thing: the return to the unchecked private monopoly power of the Coolidge epoch.

All the gentlemen whom I have named want somehow to keep the profit system. Socialism means to abolish that system. Those who want to keep it will soon find that out of war or out of the fresh economic collapse inevitable when business prosperity is so spotty, so temporary, so insecure as it is today, will come the confusion to which capitalism's final answer must be the Fascist dictator.

In America that dictator will probably not call himself Fascist. He, like Mr. Roosevelt in his address to Congress, will thank God that we are not like other nations. But privately he will rejoice in the weakness of our opposition to tyranny. Under the forms of democracy we have not preserved liberty. It has not taken black shirts, [party militants], to make us docile.

Given the crisis of war or economic collapse we, unless we awake, will accept dictatorship by violence to perpetuate a while longer the class division of income. We shall acknowledge the religion of the totalitarian state and become hypnotized by the emotional appeal of a blind jingoistic nationalism. Against this Fascist peril and its Siamese twin, the menace of war, there is no protection in the New Deal, no protection in the Republican party, less than no protection in the Liberty League.

Capitalism Does Not Protect the Common Good

Who of them all is waging a real battle even for such civil liberties and such democratic rights as ostensibly are possible in a bourgeois democracy? When Al Smith appeals to the Constitution is he thinking of the liberties of the Bill of Rights or is he thinking of the protection the Constitution has given to property?

As a Socialist I was no lover of NRA [National Recovery Act] or AAA. NRA, at least temporarily, did give the workers some encouragement to organize, but at bottom it was an elaborate scheme for the stabilization of capitalism under associations of industries which could regulate production in order to maintain profit. AAA was perhaps some relative help to many classes of farmers. It was no help at all to the most exploited agricultural workers and share-croppers, but rather the opposite. And it was, as indeed it had to be under capitalism, primarily a scheme for subsidizing scarcity.

The New Deal did not say, as socialism would have said: "Here are so many millions of American people who need to be well fed and well clothed. How much food and cotton do we require?" We should have required more, not less. What Mr. Roosevelt said was: "How much food and cotton can be produced for which the exploited masses must pay a higher price?"

This was not primarily the fault of AAA. It was the fault of the capitalist system which Roosevelt and Smith alike accept; that system which makes private profit its god, which uses planning, in so far as it uses planning at all, to stabilize and maintain the profits of private owners, not the well-being of the masses. In the last analysis the profit system inevitably depends upon relative scarcity. Without this relative scarcity there is no profit and there is no planning for abundance which accepts the kingship of private profit.

When the world went in for great machinery operated by power it went in for specialization and integration of work. It doomed the old order of the pioneers. The one chance of using machinery for life, not death, is that we should plan to use it for the common good. There is no planned production for use rather than for the private profit of an owning class which does not involve social ownership. This is the gospel of socialism.

We can have abundance. In 1929, according to the Brookings Institute—and that, remember, was our most prosperous year—a decent use of our capacity to produce would have enabled us to raise the income of the 16,400,000 families with less than $2,000 a year to that modest level without even cutting any at the top.

Instead, without any interference from workers, without any pressure from agitators, the capitalist system so dear to Al Smith and his Liberty League friends went into a nose-spin. The earned income dropped from $83,000,000,000 to something like $38,000,000,000 in 1932, and the temporary recovery, of which the New Deal administration boasts, has probably not yet raised that income to the $50,000,000,000 level. It has, moreover, burdened us with an intolerable load of debt.

The Goals of Socialism

What we must have is a society where we can use our natural resources and machinery so that the children of the share-croppers who raise cotton will no longer lack the cotton necessary for underclothes. What we must have is a society which can use our resources and our mechanical skill so that the children of builders will not live in shacks and slums.

It is not that Socialists want less private property. We want more private property in the good things of life. We do not mean to take the carpenter's kit away from the carpenter or Fritz Kreisler's violin away from Fritz Kreisler, or the home or farm in which any man lives and works away from him.

We do intend to end private landlordism, and to take the great natural resources—oil, copper, coal, iron; the great public utilities, power, transportation; the banking system, the distributive agencies like the dairy trust, the basic monopolies and essential manufacturing enterprises out of the hands of private owners, most of them absentee owners, for whose profits workers with hand and brain are alike exploited. And we intend to put these things into the hands of society.

With all the handicaps of capitalist loyalties, society has done a pretty fair job with schools, roads, waterworks and the like. Consumers' cooperatives have succeeded even in America. Social ownership now has a better record than holding company collectivism has made.

We intend to make this change to social ownership in orderly fashion. In the meantime we can avert fresh economic collapse by the road of crazy inflation or cruel deflation only by an orderly process of taxing wealth in private hands, by a graduated tax, approaching expropriation of unearned millions, in order to wipe out debt and to help in the socialization of industry.

We do not mean to turn socialized industries over to political bureaucrats, to Socialist Jim [James A.] Farleys, [postmaster general and chairman of the Democratic Party's National Committee], so to speak. The adjective doesn't redeem the noun. For instance, we intend that a socialized steel industry shall be managed under a directorate representing the workers, including, of course, the technicians in that industry, and the consumers.

We intend to put over these socialized industries a national economic planning council, a kind of council of war in the holy war against poverty. This council will represent different branches of agricultural and industrial production. It will carry out the large policies for social well-being that the Congress may determine.

It can do it without conscription and without rationing our people. We ought not to pay the price Russia has paid because we are far more industrially advanced than was Russia and should learn from Russia's mistakes as well as her successes.

Many of the functions of this national planning board will have to become genuinely international or world-wide if we are to preserve peace. It is only in a family of nations where there is something like fair play in respect to the allocation of raw materials and in the establishment of industrial standards for workers that we can hope for lasting peace. It is this peace that we seek.

Our goal, Mr. Smith, is true democracy. It is we who lead in the fight for liberty and justice which you in recent years have sadly ignored. It is we who seek to make freedom and democracy constitutional by advocating a Workers Rights' Amendment in the interest of farmers, workers and consumers, giving to Congress power to adopt all needful social and economic legislation, but leaving to the courts their present power to help protect civil and religious liberty.

Our present judicial power of legislation is as undemocratic as it is in the long run dangerous to peace. Remember the Dred Scott decision! Congress rather than the States must act because these issues are national. The religion of the Constitution with the Supreme Court as the high priests and the Liberty League as its preacher will never satisfy human hunger for freedom, peace and plenty.

The Constitution was made for man and not man for the Constitution. We Socialists seek now its orderly amendment. We seek now genuine social security, real unemployment insurance. We seek now a policy which will make it a little harder for American business interests to involve us in war as a result of a mad chase after the profits of war.

These, gentlemen who quarrel over the way to save capitalism, are the things of our immediate desire. But deepest of all is our desire for a federation of cooperative Commonwealths. Some of you may like this far less than you like the New Deal, but will you not agree that it is not the New Deal?

You said, Mr. Smith, in a peroration worthy of your old enemy, William Randolph Hearst, that there can be only one victory, of the Constitution.

And this is our reply: There is only one victory worth the seeking by the heirs of the American Revolution. It is the victory of a fellowship of free men, using government as their servant, to harness our marvelous machinery for abundance, not poverty; peace, not war; freedom, not exploitation.

This is the victory in which alone is practicable deliverance from the house of our bondage. This is the victory to which we dedicate ourselves.

GREAT
SPEECHES
IN
HISTORY

The Legacies of the Great Depression

Securing the Future of Working Americans

Frances Perkins

Frances Perkins was a teacher and social worker who became the first woman appointed to a Cabinet post, serving as Franklin D. Roosevelt's secretary of labor from 1933 to 1945. Before her appointment, Perkins served as executive secretary of the Consumers' League of New York, where she successfully lobbied for improved wages and working conditions for women and children. In 1919, Governor Alfred E. Smith appointed Perkins to New York State's Industrial Commission, and in 1929, while governor of New York, Roosevelt appointed Perkins the state's industrial commissioner. Both before and during the Great Depression, Perkins advocated unemployment insurance and pushed for a minimum wage and maximum workweek. While secretary of labor, she urged the creation of the Civilian Conservation Corps to provide work for depression-stricken youth and helped draft the Social Security Act, which was signed into law on August 14, 1935.

In the following speech broadcast over the radio on September 2, 1935, Perkins describes the Social Security Act and its benefits for the American people. Perkins explains that the act provides several state-administered, federally funded programs to protect hard-working Americans and their families. The act provides unemployment insurance for men and women who are willing, but unable to work, old-age pensions for the elderly, and wel-

Frances Perkins, "The Social Security Act," radio address, September 2, 1935.

fare benefits for the disabled. According to Perkins, the benefits received will not only increase the purchasing power of workers and thus stimulate the economy, but will secure the future of America's workers.

P eople who work for a living in the United States of America can join with all other good citizens on this forty-eighth anniversary of Labor Day in satisfaction that the Congress has passed the Social Security Act. This Act establishes unemployment insurance as a substitute for haphazard methods of assistance in periods when men and women willing and able to work are without jobs. It provides for old-age pensions which mark great progress over the measures upon which we have hitherto depended in caring for those who have been unable to provide for the years when they no longer can work. It also provides security for dependent and crippled children, mothers, the indigent disabled and the blind.

Old people who are in need, unemployables, children, mothers and the sightless, will find systematic regular provisions for needs. The Act limits the Federal aid to not more than $15 per month for the individual, provided the State in which he resides appropriates a like amount. There is nothing to prevent a State from contributing more than $15 per month in special cases and there is no requirement to allow as much as $15 from either State or Federal funds when a particular case has some personal provision and needs less than the total allowed.

Following essentially the same procedure, the Act as passed provides for Federal assistance to the States in caring for the blind, a contribution by the State of up to $15 a month to be matched in turn by a like contribution by the Federal Government. The Act also contains provision for assistance to the States in providing payments to dependent children under sixteen years of age. There also is provision in the Act for cooperation with medical and health organizations charged with rehabilitation of physically handicapped children. The necessity for adequate service in the fields of public and maternal health and child welfare calls for the extension of these services to meet individual community needs.

Old-Age Benefits

Consider for a moment those portions of the Act which, while they will not be effective this present year, yet will exert a profound and far-reaching effect upon millions of citizens. I refer to the provision for a system of old-age benefits supported by the contributions of employer and employees, and to the section which sets up the initial machinery for unemployment insurance.

Old-age benefits in the form of monthly payments are to be paid to individuals who have worked and contributed to the insurance fund in direct proportion to the total wages earned by such individuals in the course of their employment subsequent to 1936. The minimum monthly payment is to be $10, the maximum $85. These payments will begin in the year 1942 and will be to those who have worked and contributed.

Because of difficulty of administration not all employments are covered in this plan at this time so that the law is not entirely complete in coverage, but it is sufficiently broad to cover all normally employed industrial workers.

As an example of the practical operation of the old-age benefit system, consider for a moment a typical young man of thirty-five years of age, and let us compute the benefits which will accrue to him. Assuming that his income will average $100 per month over the period of thirty years until he reaches the age of sixty-five, the benefit payments due him from the insurance fund will provide him with $42.50 per month for the remainder of his life. If he has been fortunate enough to have an income of $200 per month, his income will subsequently be $61.25 per month. In the event that death occurs prior to the age of sixty-five, 3½% of the total wages earned by him subsequent to 1936 will be returned to his dependents. If death occurs after the age of sixty-five, his dependents receive the same amount, less any benefits paid to him during his lifetime.

This vast system of old-age benefits requires contributions both by employer and employee, each to contribute 3%

of the total wage paid to the employee. This tax, collected by
the Bureau of Internal Revenue, will be graduated, ranging
from 1% in 1937 to the maximum 3% in 1939 and thereafter. That is, on this man's average income of $100 a month
he will pay to the usual fund $3 a month and his employer
will also pay the same amount over his working years.

Unemployment Insurance

In conjunction with the system of old-age benefits, the Act
recognizes that unemployment insurance is an integral part
of any plan for the economic security of millions of gainfully
employed workers. It provides for a plan of cooperative
Federal-State action by which a State may enact an insurance
system, compatible with Federal requirements and best
suited to its individual needs.

The Federal Government attempts to promote and effec-
tuate these State systems, by levying a uniform Federal payroll tax of 3% on employers employing eight or more workers, with the proviso that an employer who contributes to a
State unemployment compensation system will receive a
credit of 90% of this Federal tax. After 1937, additional
credit is also allowable to any employer who, because of favorable employment experience or adequate reserves, is permitted by the State to reduce his payments.

In addition, the Act provides that after the current fiscal
year the Federal Government allocate annually to the States
$49,000,000 solely for the administration of their respective
insurance systems, thus assuring that all money paid for State
unemployment compensation will be reserved for the purpose
of compensation to the worker. It has been necessary, at the
present time, to eliminate essentially the same groups from
participation under the unemployment insurance plan as in
the old-age benefit plan, though it is possible that at some future time a more complete coverage will be formulated.

The State of New York, at the present time, has a system
of unemployment compensation which might well illustrate
the salient factors desired in such a plan; in the event of unemployment, the worker is paid 50% of his wages weekly for
a period not exceeding 16 weeks in any 52 weeks. This pay-

ment begins within three weeks after the advent of actual unemployment. California, Washington, Utah and New Hamp-
shire have passed unemployment insurance laws in recent
months and Wisconsin's law is already in effect. Thirty-five
States have old-age pension statutes and mothers' pension
acts are in force in all but three States.

With the States rests now the responsibility of devising
and enacting measures which will result in the maximum
benefits to the American workman in the field of unemployment compensation. I am confident that impending State action will not fail to take cognizance of this responsibility. The
people of the different States favor the program designed to
bring them greater security in the future and their legislatures
will speedily pass appropriate laws so that all may help to
promote the general welfare.

Federal legislation was framed in the thought that the attack upon the problems of insecurity should be a cooperative
venture participated in by both the Federal and State Governments, preserving the benefits of local administration and
national leadership. It was thought unwise to have the Federal Government decide all questions of policy and dictate
completely what the States should do. Only very necessary
minimum standards are included in the Federal measure leaving wide latitude to the States.

While the different State laws on unemployment insurance must make all contributions compulsory, the States, in
addition to deciding how these contributions shall be levied,
have freedom in determining their own waiting periods,
benefit rates, maximum benefit periods and the like. Care
should be taken that these laws do not contain benefit provisions in excess of collections. While unemployment varies
greatly in different States, there is no certainty that States
which have had less normal unemployment heretofore will
in the future have a more favorable experience than the average for the country.

It is obvious that in the best interests of the worker, industry and society, there must be a certain uniformity of standards. It is obvious, too, that we must prevent the penalizing
of competitive industry in any State which plans the early
adoption of a sound system of unemployment insurance, and

provide effective guarantees against the possibility of industry in one State having an advantage over that of another. This the uniform Federal tax does, as it costs the employer the same whether he pays the levy to the Federal Government or makes a contribution to a State unemployment insurance fund. The amount of the tax itself is a relative assurance that benefits will be standardized in all States, since under the law the entire collection must be spent on benefits to unemployed.

A Sound and Reasonable Plan

The social security measure looks primarily to the future and is only a part of the Administration's plan to promote sound and stable economic life. We cannot think of it as disassociated from the Government's program to save the homes, the farms, the businesses and banks of the Nation, and especially must we consider it a companion measure to the Works Relief Act which does undertake to provide immediate increase in employment and corresponding stimulation to private industry by purchase of supplies.

While it is not anticipated as a complete remedy for the abnormal conditions confronting us at the present time, it is designed to afford protection for the individual against future major economic vicissitudes. It is a sound and reasonable plan and framed with due regard for the present state of economic recovery. It does not represent a complete solution of the problems of economic security, but it does represent a substantial, necessary beginning. It has been developed after careful and intelligent consideration of all the facts and all of the programs that have been suggested or applied anywhere.

Few legislative proposals have had as careful study, as thorough and conscientious deliberation, as that which went into the preparation of the social security programs. It is embodied in perhaps the most useful and fundamental single piece of Federal legislation in the interest of wage earners in the United States. As President Roosevelt said when he signed the measure: "If the Senate and House of Representatives in their long and arduous session had done nothing more than pass this bill, the session would be regarded as historic for all time."

This is truly legislation in the interest of the national welfare. We must recognize that if we are to maintain a healthy economy and thriving production, we need to maintain the standard of living of the lower income groups of our population who constitute ninety per cent of our purchasing power. The President's Committee on Economic Security, of which I had the honor to be chairman, in drawing up the plan, was convinced that its enactment into law would not only carry us a long way toward the goal of economic security for the individual, but also a long way toward the promotion and stabilization of mass purchasing power without which the present economic system cannot endure.

That this intimate connection between the maintenance of mass purchasing power through a system of protection of the individual against major economic hazards is not theoretical is evidenced by the fact that England has been able to withstand the effects of the world-wide depression, even though her prosperity depends so largely upon foreign trade. English economists agree with employers and workers that this ability to weather adverse conditions has been due in no small part to social insurance benefits and regular payments which have served to maintain necessary purchasing power.

Our social security program will be a vital force working against the recurrence of severe depressions in the future. We can, as the principle of sustained purchasing power in hard times makes itself felt in every shop, store and mill, grow old without being haunted by the spectre of a poverty-ridden old age or of being a burden on our children.

The costs of unemployment compensation and old-age insurance are not actually additional costs. In some degree they have long been borne by the people, but irregularly, the burden falling much more heavily on some than on others, and none of such provisions offering an orderly or systematic assurance to those in need. The years of depression have brought home to all of us that unemployment entails huge costs to government, industry and the public alike.

Unemployment insurance will within a short time considerably lighten the public burden of caring for those unemployed. It will materially reduce relief costs in future years. In essence, it is a method by which reserves are built up during periods of employment from which compensation is paid to the unemployed in periods when work is lacking.

The passage of this act with so few dissenting votes and with so much intelligent public support is deeply significant of the progress which the American people have made in thought in the social field and awareness of methods of using cooperation through government to overcome social hazards against which the individual alone is inadequate.

During the fifteen years I have been advocating such legislation as this I have learned that the American people want such security as the law provides. It will make this great Republic a better and a happier place in which to live—for us, our children and our children's children. It is a profound and sacred satisfaction to have had some part in securing this great boon to the people of our country.

A Legacy of Wasteful Government Spending

Harry F. Byrd

Harry F. Byrd was the owner of an apple orchard and a
newspaper publisher who rose through Virginia politics
to become the state's governor and eventually a U.S. senator in 1933. Although a Democrat who initially supported President Franklin D. Roosevelt, Byrd became a
chief rival of liberal Democratic leaders throughout his
Senate career. He opposed civil rights, social programs,
and federal spending. As a champion of states' rights,
Byrd opposed the increasing size and power of the federal
government and was especially critical of Roosevelt's
New Deal legislation and the federal spending this legislation encouraged. He continued his opposition to big government and federal spending until he resigned his seat in
1964, replaced by his son, Harry F. Byrd Jr.

The following speech, delivered before the Massachusetts Federation of Taxpayers in 1938, attacks the wasteful
spending policies of the Roosevelt administration. Byrd argues that spending money on relief not only corrupts
American workers, but takes away from the authority
given by the U.S. Constitution to the states. Byrd questions
the economic policy of chairman of the Federal Reserve
Board Marriner Eccles, who argues that federal spending
will stimulate the economy. The public debt has become so
large, says Byrd, that balancing the budget should be a
government priority. According to Byrd, efficiency, not
wasteful spending, will ensure America's security.

Harry F. Byrd, "National Financial Preparedness: The Brain-Trusters Should Go
Home," address to the Massachusetts Federation of Taxpayers Association,
Boston, Massachusetts, December 10, 1938.

I t is a particular honor and a particular pleasure for a Virginian to be permitted to address this distinguished gathering of Massachusetts citizens. I am delighted to come here as the guest of the Massachusetts Federation of Taxpayers, whose constructive work is well known to me. Today nothing is more important than to bring to the citizens of our nation a true understanding of the complex administration of our governments and baptize ourselves afresh in the pure principles of representative democracy. . . .

The sacred responsibility of preserving representative democracy rests upon the shoulders of American citizens because here it has flowered to the fullest perfection in freedom and in our progress and our development. Preserve it not only for ourselves and Americans who come after us, but as an inspiration and encouragement to the depressed peoples in other lands who seek the blessings of the freedom we enjoy here.

Democracy must be made efficient. Democracy must be made effective to meet conditions and new problems, but this, and all of this, can be accomplished within the framework of our constitutional government, and preserve as a continuing vital force the fundamental principles which are just as valid today as ever before. . . .

For the past several years we have had at Washington much loose talk and loose thinking of a new liberalism which will sweep away the clouds of depression; wave a magic wand of legislative panaceas for our ills and give a substitute for those time-old virtues of thrift, frugality, self-reliance and industry that have made our country great and given to us a progress, a freedom, a happiness, a contentment that has never before been enjoyed by any great nation. From my own personal observation in the Senate of the United States, a modern liberal is tested and judged in proportion as to how liberal he is willing to be with other people's money. If a senator votes to squander the people's money for every fantastic spending scheme devised in the human mind, he is a great liberal. If a senator acts to safe-guard the public treasury, to spend the taxpayers' money judiciously, and only for necessary and useful functions, he is proclaimed a "reactionary," "an economic royalist," and more recently a "copperhead."

Calling names never solved a problem or offered a solution for difficulties. For myself, how I am classified in the public life of America is of little concern to me. I am a Democrat. I have voted my convictions and owe my allegiance to my constituents of Virginia and to my oath as a senator of the United States. I intend to take orders from no man, no matter how powerful he may be. I prefer to be a "Yes, but, Senator" to a "Yes, yes, Senator.". . . .

Evaluating the Legislation

Today the time has come to analyze, to appraise the good as well as the bad, and to pass judgment on the vast legislation adopted by the National Congress in the past six years. Our last election indicates very clearly that the American people intend to do this very thing, and are doing it. In this analysis let us remember that the real test of a law—the real worth of legislation—is in practical administration and effect upon all the millions of our citizens, and that a principle enacted into a law—a just and fair principle—is often defeated by the maladministration of its operation.

With much important legislation enacted in this period, I can heartily agree. I have been in accord with the foreign policies of our government. I have supported Secretary Cordell Hull in his efforts to regain our foreign trade and to repair some of the damage of the Hawley-Smoot Tariff Bill signed by President Hoover. I have supported adequate national defense and will continue to do so unless national defense is used merely as a means of pump priming and public spending. I favored control of the New York Stock Exchange and will vote for greater control to eliminate existing abuses. I am opposed to monopolies that operate to throttle competition and fix prices. I applaud the remarkably fine work done in the reorganization of the banking system. As a member of a Special Committee of the Finance Committee to consider a revision of the social security legislation, I will support measures to reform and strengthen and make workable a social security program within the ability of our citizenship to support. Social security, in one form or another, is here to stay.

In surveying recent legislation, remember that private enterprise is the foundation stone on which our Republic is founded. Private enterprise, and not the government, must provide employment for our citizens. Private enterprise is the motor that provides the taxes for our government to operate. If taxes become confiscatory, if governmental regimentation becomes too oppressive, if governmental competition becomes too destructive, then private enterprise can neither pay the taxes nor give employment to the workers. Remember too that the character of our individual citizen is our most valuable national possession, and the character of many can and will be injured, if not destroyed, by unrestricted and profligate public relief, as character comes from self-help and industry and not from idleness and thriftlessness. The very immensity of our relief expenditures has made impractical the confinement of relief to those actually in need—an obligation that all of us recognize must be met in the fullest measure—with the result that millions of able-bodied citizens rely upon the government for support and have ceased to exert their effort for self-help and to obtain private employment.

A grant to the states by the Federal government is not a gift. Nothing would curb the wanton extravagance in our Federal government more than a recognition of this very simple and elementary principle. Actually every grant from the Federal government in the past five years has in fact been a mortgage, and a first mortgage, on the property of every citizen in each of the 48 states. In this confederation of states— United States of America—the parent government has no money except such as is derived from the states by taxation. It has no security on which to borrow except the property of the citizens of the 48 states, so instead of a grant being a gift, the states are given a mortgage to pay with accrued interest, and the bureaucrats at Washington take a toll for top-heavy administrative cost, which, in some instances, as I have shown on the floor of the Senate, has equaled a full 33 per cent of the sum expended.

A Wasteful Government

As one who for three years has been investigating our federal expenditures as Chairman of the Select Committee on

Investigation of Executive Agencies of the Government, I assert that we have at Washington today the most costly, the most wasteful and most bureaucratic form of government this Republic has ever known or any other nation has been afflicted with.

For nine years we have spent more than our income for recovery and relief. Our deficit for the current fiscal year will be the largest in peace-time history. For recovery and relief we have spent $27,000,000,000 since the depression began. In addition, we have borrowed and loaned $8,000,000,000 more to citizens and corporations, much of which, I predict, will never be repaid to our government. Our debt in 1932 was $16,000,000,000, with no contingent liabilities. On July 1, next, we will owe at least $41,000,000,000 in direct debt and will have a contingent liability, which is not listed on the financial statements of the government and of which no government official has made announcement. This liability is just as much an obligation as the reported debt. Thirty government corporations have been organized with authority to issue bonds, debentures and notes to the amount of $16,229,325,000. These obligations when issued are guaranteed in full for principal and interest by the government of the United States, but I repeat are not included in the debt you find reported in the Treasury statements. With much difficulty, I have ascertained that on June 1, last, bonds, debentures and notes had been issued by these corporations, over three-fourths having been sold to the public to the amount of $7,940,462,000, so that our actual debt on July 1, next, will approach $50,000,000,000. . . .

Our situation today, in brief, is this:

We have trebled the public debt in five years. This debt is now an average of over $1,000,000,000 for each state, and the interest before this debt is paid will be more than the debt itself. The federal appropriations in this current year are the largest in peace-time history. Our tax collections for the year ending last July were the largest. Yet in the present fiscal year our deficit will be the largest peace-time deficit. In the ninth consecutive year of great deficits, we are farther away—and I say this advisedly—farther away from a balanced budget than at any time since the depression began.

The Federal government alone is spending $23,000 every minute of every day and every night including Sunday, and of this $11,500 is being added each minute to the public debt.

Coincident with the rise in the federal debt and increase in federal taxation have come similar increases in the burdens of the states and localities. The Federal government has demanded the same prodigality of spending by the other governmental units of our Republic, and the sovereign state of Georgia has only recently been publicly reprimanded because that state was reluctant to amend its constitution to issue state bonds and abandon its wise and frugal policy of pay-as-you-go.

This current year, the fiscal year of 1939, the expenditures of all governments in America will be more than $20,000,000,000, or about one-third of the total gross income of this nation, and this $20,000,000,000 is more than twice the value of all products that come from the soil and under the ground, all the products of the farm; including livestock, the products of the forest and the products of the mines. How long can a Republic exist spending one-third of its gross income and twice the value of the new wealth that comes from the soil? . . .

A Perilous Situation

We are facing a perilous situation and what can be done about it? Can we expect any leadership from the present administration for economy and retrenchment? As one who has fought for five years for prudent spending at Washington, I say no. As a Democrat I say it with sorrow, as my party is in power, but the Republican party cannot escape responsibility for their share in the present orgy of spending. Mr. Hoover added the first five billions to the public debt and a majority of the Republican members in the Senate have voted for the huge appropriation bills.

So long as the economic philosophy of such men as Chairman [Marriner] Eccles of the Federal Reserve Board dominates the fiscal policies of the present administration, no leadership from those in high places in Washington to restore the country to a sane budget policy can be hoped for. Mr. Eccles, one of the sponsors of the discredited undivided profits tax, repealed by public demand, believes that government spending should be regulated not by the needs in the functions of government, but for the purpose of promoting prosperity by spending borrowed money. The more you borrow and spend, the more prosperous you are; the more taxes you pay, the more prosperous you are, says Mr. Eccles. This incredible statement was made by the head of our National Banking system in New York last week and indicates to what depths of false reasoning we have sunk in the crack-pot legislative ideas of those holding important public positions. "It is perilous," says Mr. Eccles, "to reduce public spending," and to adopt sound principles of financing after nine years of fiscal insanity. I say it is not only perilous if we do not start soon to approach a balanced budget, but it will be disastrous. What about the hardships and distress we will suffer when the pay day comes and our sweat and toil must pay for this reckless waste, not only to repay the principal of the debt, but for the interest?

If federal spending is a prop for prosperity, what will happen when the prop is withdrawn, as some day must be done because not even the richest nation in the world can continue indefinitely to violate the basic principles of sound finance? We have primed the pump with borrowed money for five years. The result has been a tragic failure. Our unemployment today, as just announced by the government, is over 10,500,000, or 3,000,000 more than a year ago, and not so many less than when the depression began.

Mr. Eccles further said in New York that the recession that began in the fall of 1937 was caused by reduced public spending. The actual records contradict this statement. For the year beginning July 1, 1937, all governments—local, state and national—spent $18,415,000,000, and for the previous year $17,516,000,000. So we spent more and not less. Mr. Eccles said again that taxes in America were 17½ per cent of the national income and 20 per cent in England, and cited this as one of the reasons why the business index in England is now 118 per cent of the 1929 level and in the United States 75 per cent. He omitted to say that England is on a pay-as-you-go basis and that while our tax collections this year are

17½ per cent of our income, our actual expenditures for all governments totalled 30 per cent, or 10 per cent more than in England. Following this line of reasoning, then our prosperity should be greater than England's prosperity, but Mr. Eccles says it is not.

To my way of thinking, Mr. Eccles paid a tribute in this comparison to pay-as-you-go financing. If Great Britain can reduce her public debt per capita, as she has done, for the past five years, and have a relatively higher prosperity than we have, then a pay-as-you-go plan in this country may bring to us the advantages that Great Britain now apparently enjoys.

Under the pay-as-you-go plan England has reduced her per capita taxation 5 per cent as compared to the levies of 1928. Our Federal government has increased the per capita taxation in the same period by 22 per cent and is paying by taxation only one dollar out of each two dollars expended. . . .

The vast federal spending is entrenched in every nook and corner of America. Actually one out of every 80 men, women and children in the United States is now on the regular payroll, as more than one million and a half are regularly employed by the Federal government in its various activities. In addition, there are more than one million federal pensioners, and to this must be added the millions receiving federal relief and subsidies of one kind or another. To dismantle and reduce this gigantic bureaucracy is a task of overwhelming proportions, but the reward is the preservation of sound government and to prevent inflation and keep our country secure for our children and those to follow.

A Plan to Reduce Government Spending

Let me suggest a program:

First thoroughly reorganize the Federal government for simplification, retrenchment and economy, and I propose to introduce such legislation.

With equal emphasis I submit there should be a cancellation of the existing authority of 30 federal borrowing corporations which now have power to add $8,000,000,000 to the public debt; and that such corporations, about which so little is known, should function through the budget, allowing

Congress to approve or reject future expenditures. This action would preclude at least a portion of the enormous public debt now impending.

Inescapable in this program is the fact that, exclusive of relief, 30 per cent of the total expended by the government today is for activities new to the government in the last five years (the Greenbelts, and tree belts, and other such dispensable activities). Let these be reduced to the minimum and great sums can be saved without impairing the necessary functions of government.

This program would embrace a thorough, honest purge of relief rolls eliminating all undeserving, and reducing relief costs by stopping all expenditures in excess of providing for those in need; and this can only be done by requiring localities to bear a portion of the burden, thereby directing local interest to reform in the relief program. Elimination of unnecessary relief costs is vital to the preservation of the character of the American people.

It is a fact that 33 states take from the Federal government for relief (exclusive of grants and subsidies) more than they pay into the Treasury from which they draw. Virginia and Massachusetts are among the 15 states in all the nation with relief drafts on the Federal government of less than they contribute in revenue.

Reasonable taxation is one of the best assurances of business prosperity. The essence of our Democracy is the conducting of our government within the ability of our people to pay.

Government efficiently and economically operated is our best protection against the undermining of democracy.

National financial preparedness would be the objective of this program. Financial preparedness is the greatest bulwark of national defense, and it is the greatest guarantee for national security.

The Principles of Democracy Are Still at Work

Charles Evans Hughes

As chief justice of the Supreme Court, Charles Evans
Hughes gained respect for balancing the conservative and
progressive forces that clashed during the Great Depression. Hughes served as governor of New York from 1906
to 1920 and was first nominated to the U.S. Supreme
Court by President Taft in 1910. He left the Court in
1916 to run for president against Woodrow Wilson and
served as secretary of state under Presidents Warren
Harding and Calvin Coolidge. President Herbert Hoover
named Hughes chief justice of the U.S. Supreme Court in
1930. Hughes generally favored the exercise of federal
power, although he invalidated the National Industrial
Recovery Act, one of the principal New Deal statutes of
Franklin D. Roosevelt's administration. However, with
the threat of Roosevelt's plan to "pack" the Supreme
Court by increasing the number of justices and appointing new, liberal Justices to replace those over seventy who
refused to retire, the Court began to uphold provisions of
the Social Security Act. Many believe these decisions contributed to the defeat of the court-packing bill.

On March 4, 1939, Hughes, seventy-seven at the
time of his address, spoke before a Joint Session of the
Senate and House of Representatives to celebrate the
Sesquicentennial. In his historic speech, Hughes claims
that despite expansion and economic change, the democratic principles on which the nation was founded remain

Charles Evans Hughes, address to the joint session of the U.S. Senate and U.S.
House of Representatives, Washington, D.C., March 4, 1939.

intact. By maintaining a balance between centralized authority and local autonomy, says Hughes, America's representative government has withstood the threat of autocracy. The Supreme Court balances the needs of
government with the rights of the individual, but by
keeping to its own functions, Hughes tells those gathered
before him in the House, each department of the government secures the promise of life, liberty, and the pursuit
of happiness for the American people.

Hughes retired from the Court in 1941 at the age of
seventy-nine.

T he most significant fact in connection with this anniversary is that, after 150 years, notwithstanding expansion of territory, enormous increase in population,
and profound economic changes, despite direct attack and
subversive influences, there is every indication that the vastly
preponderant sentiment of the American people is that our
form of government shall be preserved. . . .

Forms of government, however well contrived, cannot as-
sure their own permanence. If we owe to the wisdom and restraint of the [founding] fathers a system of government which
has thus far stood the test, we all recognize that it is only by
wisdom and restraint in our own day that we can make that
system last. If today we find ground for confidence that our
institutions which have made for liberty and strength will be
maintained, it will not be due to abundance of physical resources or to productive capacity, but because these are at the
command of a people who still cherish the principles which
underlie our system, and because of the general appreciation
of what is essentially sound in our governmental structure.

With respect to the influences which shape public opinion, we live in a new world. Never have these influences operated more directly, or with such variety of facile instruments, or with such overwhelming force. We have mass
production in opinion as well as in goods. The grasp of tradition and of sectional prejudgment is loosened. Postulates of
the past must show cause. Our institutions will not be pre-

served by veneration of what is old, if that is simply expressed in the formal ritual of a shrine. The American people
are eager and responsive. They listen attentively to a vast
multitude of appeals and, with this receptivity, it is only upon
their sound judgment that we can base our hope for a wise
conservatism with continued progress and appropriate adap-
tation to new needs.

We shall do well on this anniversary if the thought of the
people is directed to the essentials of our democracy. Here in
this body we find the living exponents of the principle of representative government—not government by direct mass action but by representation, which means leadership as well as
responsiveness and accountability.

Preserving the Balance of Power

Here the ground swells of autocracy, destructive of parlia-
mentary independence, have not yet upset or even disturbed
the authority and responsibility of the essential legislative
branch of democratic institutions. We have a National Government equipped with vast powers which have proved to be
adequate to the development of a great nation, and at the
same time maintaining the balance between centralized authority and local autonomy. It has been said that to preserve
that balance, if we did not have States we should have to create them. In our 48 States we have the separate sources of
power necessary to protect local interests and thus also to
preserve the central authority, in the vast variety of our concerns, from breaking down under its own weight. . . .

We not only praise individual liberty but our constitutional system has the unique distinction of insuring it. Our
guarantees of fair trials, of due process in the protection of
life, liberty, and property—which stands between the citizen
and arbitrary power—of religious freedom, of free speech,
free press and free assembly, are the safeguards which have
been erected against the abuses threatened by gusts of passion and prejudice which in misguided zeal would destroy the
basic interests of democracy. We protect the fundamental
right of minorities, in order to save democratic government
from destroying itself by the excesses of its own power. The

firmest ground for confidence in the future is that more than ever we realize that, while democracy must have its organization and controls, its vital breath is individual liberty.

I am happy to be here as the representative of the tribunal which is charged with the duty of maintaining, through the decision of controversies, these constitutional guaranties. We are a separate but not an independent arm of government. You, not we, have the purse and the sword. You, not we, determine the establishment and the jurisdiction of the lower Federal courts and the bounds of the appellate jurisdiction of the Supreme Court. The Congress first assembled on March 4, 1789, and on September 24, 1789, as its twentieth enactment, passed the Judiciary Act—to establish the judicial courts of the United States—a statute which is a monument of wisdom, one of the most satisfactory acts in the long history of notable congressional legislation. It may be said to take rank in our annals as next in importance to the Constitution itself.

In thus providing the judicial establishment, and in equipping and sustaining it, you have made possible the effective functioning of the department of government which is designed to safeguard with judicial impartiality and independence the interests of liberty. But in the great enterprise of making democracy workable we are all partners. One member of our body politic cannot say to another: "I have no need of thee." We work in successful cooperation by being true, each department to its own functions, and all to the spirit which pervades our institutions, exalting the processes of reason, seeking through the very limitations of power the promotion of the wise use of power, and finding the ultimate security of life, liberty, and the pursuit of happiness, and the promise of continued stability and a rational progress in the good sense of the American people.

Appendix of Biographies

Harry F. Byrd

Harry F. Byrd was born in 1887 into a family that had arrived on Virginia's shores in 1670. The Byrd family amassed a fortune as one of the state's largest orchardists. They also owned two daily newspapers and six weeklies.

At fifteen, Byrd took over the management of the debt-ridden *Star* newspaper from his father. The *Star* owed so much to the Antietam Paper Company that the supplier threatened to cut off the delivery of newsprint. Byrd negotiated a new deal—a day's newsprint at a time, paid for on delivery. From those beginnings sprang Byrd's lifelong passion for fiscal responsibility. As governor of Virginia, for example, rather than issue bonds, Byrd instituted pay-as-you-go funding of state roads.

As a U.S. senator and member of the Senate Finance Committee, Byrd was a staunch critic of federal spending. During the depression Byrd opposed many of President Franklin D. Roosevelt's New Deal prescriptions and was a constant opponent of big government, civil rights, and social programs.

While Byrd's opponents argue he created a political machine that held back the state of Virginia, his supporters argue he maintained his power because he understood the will of the people, which allowed him to take both conservative and progressive stands on the issues. As governor, Byrd helped pass one of the most stringent antilynching laws in the country, yet he resisted federally mandated integration of schools. He remained a champion of states' rights and segregation until he retired from the Senate in 1965 and was replaced by his son Harry F. Byrd Jr. Byrd died in 1966.

Charles E. Coughlin

Known as the radio priest, Charles E. Coughlin developed one of the first loyal audiences in radio broadcast history. He had an enormous influence on depression-era America. At the height of his popularity, one-third of the nation tuned in to his weekly broadcasts. Coughlin received four hundred thousand letters a week and was featured twice on the cover of *Newsweek*.

Born in 1891, Coughlin was the son of a Great Lakes seaman. He was raised in Hamilton, Ontario, and educated at the University of Toronto's St. Michael's College. After graduation, Coughlin entered St. Basil's Seminary. He was ordained in 1916 and became pastor of the Shrine of the Little Flower in Royal Oak, Michigan, in 1926.

Father Coughlin began his radio career broadcasting sermons to children. His first broadcast, the *Golden Hour of the Little Flower*, was relayed from the parish on October 3, 1926. By the early 1930s, Coughlin's broadcasts shifted to the economic and political perils facing the country. His core message was one of economic populism, but his attacks on prominent Jewish figures made him increasingly controversial, and the Catholic Church forced him to stop his broadcasts and return to his work as a parish priest in 1940. He remained pastor of the Shrine until his retirement in 1966.

Coughlin was originally an avid supporter of President Franklin D. Roosevelt, but in 1936, when Roosevelt failed to employ radical reforms, Coughlin supported a third-party candidate and formed the National Union for Social Justice to lobby independently for his social and economic proposals. In his magazine *Social Justice*, Coughlin attacked Roosevelt, communism, Wall Street, and Jews. Coughlin also wrote several books, including *Christ or the Red Serpent* (1930), *By the Sweat of Thy Brow* (1931), and *The New Deal in Money* (1933). Coughlin died in Bloomfield Hills, Michigan, in 1979.

Hallie Flanagan

Hallie Flanagan, born in South Dakota in 1890, studied at Grinnell College in Iowa, and married while still in college. Her husband died in 1919, leaving her with two children to support. When she received her M.A. from Radcliffe in 1924, she knew she could not support a family as a playwright, so she accepted a position teaching drama at Vassar. Flanagan received a fellowship to study the theater in Europe and when she returned, founded the Vassar Experimental Theatre to introduce students to European avant-garde theater.

President Franklin D. Roosevelt lured Flanagan from Vassar to head the Federal Theatre Project (FTP). Although a government project, the FTP was Flanagan's vision, and she set a standard for theatrical production that many claim remains unmatched. According to Flanagan:

> It is our job in the Federal Theatre Project to expand, as greatly as our imagination and talents will permit, the boundaries of theater. . . . The American Theatre must wake up and grow up— wake up to an age of expanding social consciousness, an age in which men are demanding that war and social injustice be outlawed, an age in which men are whispering through space, soar-

ing to the stars, and flinging miles of steel and glass into the air.
If the plays do not exist, we shall have to write them.

In a legendary hearing before the U.S. House of Representatives
Committee on Un-American Activities, Flanagan was accused of
promoting leftist ideas, and the FTP was halted in 1939. She returned to Vassar and directed the writing of *Arena* (1940), an account of the FTP. She became dean of Smith College in 1942 and
was a professor of theater there until 1955.

Herbert Hoover

Herbert Clark Hoover was born August 10, 1874, to hardworking
parents but was orphaned at age six and raised by his aunt and uncle. The circumstances of his childhood instilled in Hoover a strong
sense of self-reliance, industriousness, and concern for the downtrodden. Hoover became a self-made millionaire after he graduated
from Stanford University with a degree in geology. With his business acumen, Hoover amassed about $4 million in mining engi-
neering projects around the globe.

Hoover served as secretary of commerce from 1921 to 1928,
and when President Calvin Coolidge decided not to run for a second term, Hoover became the Republican presidential nominee.
During the 1928 presidential campaign, Hoover told America, "We
are nearer today to the ideal of the abolition of poverty and fear
from the lives of men and women than ever before in any land."
Hoover won the election; however, in the first year of his term, the
stock market crashed, and the nation slipped into a severe depression. Hoover was unable to alleviate the unemployment, homeless-
ness, and hunger that followed, and many blamed him for the
worsening depression.

Franklin D. Roosevelt easily defeated Hoover in the 1932 election. During the time between Hoover's defeat and Roosevelt's
inauguration, Roosevelt ignored Hoover's attempts to discuss economic policy, and Hoover left the White House defeated and em-
bittered. Hoover believed that Roosevelt's New Deal mirrored European fascism and threatened democratic ideals and individual
liberty. He continued to argue his position in *The Challenge to Liberty* (1934) and *Addresses upon the American Road* (1946–1961).
Under Harry Truman and Dwight D. Eisenhower, he led the Hoover
Commission, which aimed to streamline the federal bureaucracy.

Hoover was an ardent anticommunist but opposed international
crusades. Until the Japanese attack on Pearl Harbor, he opposed
U.S. entry in World War II, and he denounced American involve-
ment in the Korean and Vietnam Wars.

Charles Evans Hughes

Charles Evans Hughes was born on April 11, 1862, in Glens Falls, New York, and received his law degree from Columbia University Law School. Before his political and judicial career, Hughes practiced law in New York City and taught at Columbia and Cornell.

Hughes came to prominence when he served as chief counsel for two joint committees of the New York State Legislature investigating gas utilities and insurance companies. His exposure of malpractice in these industries brought him the Republican nomination for governor of New York in 1906, a campaign in which he defeated the flamboyant newspaper publisher William Randolph Hearst.

In 1910, President William Howard Taft appointed Hughes associate justice of the Supreme Court, but in 1916, Hughes accepted the Republican presidential nomination and the endorsement of a Republican splinter group called the Progressive, or Bull Moose, Party. He was narrowly defeated by Woodrow Wilson, 277 electoral votes to 254. Hughes also served as secretary of state under President Warren Harding.

Despite liberal opposition in the Senate, President Herbert Hoover appointed Hughes chief justice of the Supreme Court. As chief justice, Hughes led the Court through the controversy over Franklin D. Roosevelt's New Deal legislation. Hughes generally favored the exercise of federal power, but the Court invalidated the National Industrial Recovery Act. In 1937, Roosevelt proposed to pack the Supreme Court by appointing a new liberal justice to offset each sitting justice over the age of seventy who refused to retire. Hughes vehemently attacked the proposed law. However, under Hughes's direction, the Court sustained some New Deal legislation such as the right to collective bargaining through the Wagner Act of 1935 and a few weeks later upheld various provisions of the Social Security Act.

Hughes was a superb communicator. His realistic approach, a blend of conservation of basic principles with a recognition of the need for change, enabled him to enhance consensus on fundamental issues. He retired in 1941.

Robert Maynard Hutchins

Robert Maynard Hutchins was born January 17, 1899, in Brooklyn, New York. Hutchins graduated from Yale University Law School in 1925, becoming its dean in 1927. At the young age of thirty, Hutchins became the president of the University of Chicago, where he began a controversial career as administrator.

Hutchins believed the education available at even the most prestigious of American universities was inadequate: "Our erroneous notion of progress had thrown the classics and the liberal arts out of the curriculum, overemphasized the empirical sciences, and made education the servant of any contemporary movements in society, no matter how superficial." His Chicago Plan encouraged liberal education rather than specialization. He believed the role of the college should be to provide all students the same general curriculum in the first years of college and argued that comprehensive examination should measure achievement rather than classroom time attended. Hutchins sought to balance the college curriculum and to maintain the Western intellectual tradition, introducing the systematic study of "great" books.

Hutchins vigorously defended academic freedom, opposing faculty loyalty oaths in the 1950s. In 1959, Hutchins founded the Center for the Study of Democratic Institutions in Santa Barbara, California, which hoped to approach Hutchins's ideal of a community of scholars discussing a wide range of issues, including individual freedom, international order, ecological imperatives, the rights of minorities and women, and the nature of the good life.

From 1943 until his retirement in 1974, Hutchins was chair of the board of editors of *Encyclopaedia Britannica* and the editor in chief of the fifty-four-volume *Great Books of the Western World* (1952).

John L. Lewis

John L. Lewis was born in Lucas, Iowa, and went to work in the coal mines at age sixteen. His grandiloquent oratory made Lewis an effective leader, and over fifty-seven years, Lewis lifted himself from the coal mines to a prominent and controversial position in the labor movement.

Famed for his bushy eyebrows and fiery rhetoric, Lewis served as president of the United Mine Workers of America (UMWA) from 1920 until 1960. During the depression years, Lewis worked to organize the country's industrial workers through the Congress of Industrial Organizations (CIO), which helped raise living standards for millions of American families. In the first year of the CIO, nearly 4 million workers joined labor organizations and wages were raised by over a billion dollars. In 1933, Lewis sent hundreds of UMWA organizers to help create some of the nation's leading labor unions, including the United Steelworkers of America (USWA), the United Auto Workers (UAW) and the Communications Workers of America (CWA).

Lewis backed President Franklin Roosevelt in 1936, but in 1940 switched to the Republicans. In 1943, Lewis led a half-million mine workers on strike, demanding wage increases. The strike closed down steel mills for two weeks during World War II, which angered many Americans, but to miners, Lewis was a hero. "If John L. Lewis told us to go on strike tomorrow, we would go out, even if it meant going to prison for 20 years," a mine worker told the *New York Times*. His greatest legacy was the creation of the UMWA Welfare and Retirement Fund, which built eight hospitals in Appalachia and established many clinics. In 1964, President Lyndon Johnson awarded Lewis the Presidential Medal of Freedom, the nation's highest civilian decoration.

Huey Long

Born on a farm in Winnfield, Louisiana, in 1893, Huey Pierce Long became a colorful, charismatic, and controversial political leader. He gave himself the nickname "Kingfish" because, he said, "I'm a small fish here in Washington. But I'm the Kingfish to the folks down in Louisiana." A gifted student, Long passed the bar at age twenty-one after dropping out of Tulane Law School and practiced law in Shreveport. Although Long lost a lawsuit against Standard Oil, he won other compensation suits for injured workers.

Long first ran for governor in 1924 at the age of thirty. When he won the gubernatorial election on his second try in 1928, he embarked on a series of reforms that approached outright rebellion against the ruling class. An ardent enemy of corporate interests, he championed the "little man" against the rich and privileged. Long implemented an adult literacy program in Louisiana that largely served African Americans, despite the racism of the overwhelming white majority. His reforms were surprisingly progressive despite his portrayal as a despot.

Huey Long was elected to the U.S. Senate in 1930. While a senator, Long was the determined enemy of Wall Street, bankers, and big business. Because Long believed the administration of Franklin D. Roosevelt was constrained by these forces, he was a critic of many New Deal programs. A champion of the poor during the depression, Long promoted his Share-the-Wealth plan to redistribute America's wealth and created grass-roots organizations called Share-the-Wealth clubs, whose slogan was "Every Man a King." By 1935, more than 7 million people had joined Long's clubs.

Many considered Long a serious threat to the Roosevelt administration when in the spring of 1935 Long tried to unite the radical movements and form a third party. Long was so confident he would become president of the United States in 1946 that he wrote a book entitled *My First Days in the White House*. Long was assassinated, however, on September 10, 1935.

Frances Perkins

Frances Perkins was an active worker in industrial health and safety issues, especially as they affected women and children. She was also the first woman to serve a federal administration as secretary of labor. Perkins was born on April 10, 1882, in Boston, Massachusetts, to a prosperous Boston family. She graduated from Mount Holyoke College in 1902. While at Mount Holyoke, she visited many local factories and developed a permanent interest in the problems of working people and the working poor. She joined the settlement house movement in the slums of Chicago and worked with immigrant girls in Philadelphia. These early experiences sparked her mission to improve the lives of the less fortunate.

Perkins received a master's degree in social economics from Columbia University in 1910. She became executive secretary of the Consumer's League of New York City and its Committee on Safety, which made her an expert on health and safety issues. She became well known as a social worker and active lobbyist for legislative reforms.

When Franklin D. Roosevelt became president, he chose Perkins as his secretary of labor. When she accepted the position, Perkins remarked, "I came to Washington to work for God, FDR, and the millions of forgotten, plain common workingmen." She continued in office until 1945. Her main achievements include the Social Security Act of 1935, the Fair Labor Standards Act of 1938, and the Wages and Hours Act of 1938. She also supported the abolition of child labor and the establishment of the Civilian Conservation Corps.

Perkins was trained as a teacher and taught and lectured at various universities throughout her lifetime. In 1946, she published a memoir of the president, *The Roosevelt I Knew*.

Will Rogers

Will Rogers, America's cowboy philosopher, was an entertainer and writer famed for one-liners such as "I never met a man I didn't like." Rogers was born on November 4, 1879, on a large ranch in the Cherokee Nation that would later become part of Oklahoma. His father, Clem Rogers, was a successful rancher, cattleman, and banker.

Rogers was taught by a freed slave how to use a lasso, and Rogers eventually became an expert at roping skills. He took his act on the road, starring in Wild West shows and vaudeville. Dressing as a cowboy, Rogers used his folksy charm to mock himself and the public figures of his time. Audiences prized his wisecracks and folksy observations more than his expert roping; Rogers was well informed, telling the truth in simple words that everyone could understand.

Rogers's popularity made him a star of Broadway and seventy-one movies of the 1920s and 1930s. With the advent of sound he became a top box-office attraction. Rogers traveled around the globe three times, the entertainer of kings and commoners alike. He was also a popular broadcaster and wrote more than four thousand syndicated newspaper columns and six books. His broadcasts and columns often poked fun at politicians, both Democrats and Republicans. He once remarked, "Every time Congress makes a joke it's law, and every time they make a law it's a joke."

Rogers died in a plane crash near Point Barrow, Alaska, with his good friend, aviation legend Wiley Post, on August 15, 1935.

Eleanor Roosevelt

Eleanor Roosevelt was not only the wife of the thirty-second president of the United States, Franklin D. Roosevelt, but a diplomat to the United Nations and a noted humanitarian. In her time, she was one of the world's most widely admired and powerful women.

Roosevelt was born October 11, 1884, in New York City, the niece of Theodore Roosevelt. Her parents died before she was ten, and she was raised by relatives. She enrolled in a girl's boarding school outside London, where she was influenced by the French headmistress, Marie Souvestre, whose taste for travel and excellence inspired Eleanor. Once back in New York, she devoted time to community service; soon after, a distant cousin, Franklin D. Roosevelt, began to court her, and they were married on March 17, 1905. Eleanor gave birth to six children, one of whom died in infancy.

During her twelve years as first lady, the unprecedented breadth of Roosevelt's activities and her advocacy of liberal causes made her nearly as controversial as her husband. She was her husband's eyes and ears and embarked on extensive tours of the nation reporting on conditions, programs, and public opinion. She also held press conferences for women corespondents, and beginning in 1936, she wrote a daily syndicated newspaper column, "My Day," and was a widely sought-after speaker at political meetings and institutions.

Roosevelt showed a particular interest in child welfare, housing reform, and equal rights for women and racial minorities. In 1939, when the Daughters of the American Revolution refused to let African American opera singer Marian Anderson perform in Constitution Hall, Roosevelt resigned her membership and arranged to hold the concert at the nearby Lincoln Memorial; the event turned into a massive outdoor celebration attended by seventy-five thousand people. Her defense of the rights of African Americans, youth, and the poor helped bring groups into government that formerly had been alienated from the political process.

After FDR's death, President Harry S. Truman appointed Roosevelt a delegate to the United Nations, where she served as chair of the Commission on Human Rights and played a major role in the drafting and adopting of the Universal Declaration of Human Rights in 1948. In 1961, President John F. Kennedy appointed her chair of his Commission on the Status of Women, and she continued that work until shortly before her death in 1962.

Franklin Delano Roosevelt

Franklin Delano Roosevelt, the thirty-second president of the United States, was born on January 30, 1882, in Hyde Park, New York, to wealth and social position. Roosevelt was educated at Harvard University and Columbia University Law School. He admired the progressive policies of his fifth cousin, President Theodore Roosevelt, who advocated an increased role for government in economic affairs. He married Theodore Roosevelt's niece, Eleanor Roosevelt, in 1905.

Roosevelt entered politics in 1910, when he sought and won a seat in the New York State Senate. Roosevelt supported Woodrow Wilson for the presidential nomination in 1912 and was appointed assistant secretary of the navy in 1913. Roosevelt became Wilson's vice presidential nominee, but he was stricken with polio in 1921, which left him a paraplegic. Roosevelt returned to politics in 1928 and was elected governor of New York. A great speaker, he managed to disguise his disability through a series of complex strategies designed to make him appear able-bodied when he appeared in public. Roosevelt once remarked to the great Orson Welles, "Orson, you and I are the two best actors in America!"

Elected to the presidency for four consecutive terms beginning in 1932, Roosevelt helped redefine the role of government in economic affairs. He believed that the federal government should take decisive action to help farmers, laborers, and consumers. He blamed financial leaders and big business for America's economic plight and recommended government regulation of banks and industry. Roosevelt began his first term by providing relief for the unemployed and a plan to increase income for farmers. In 1934 he proposed a social security system that secured the economic future of American citizens.

Roosevelt's second term began with a struggle with the Supreme Court, which had held several of his New Deal projects unconstitutional. In retaliation Roosevelt proposed to add new justices who would approve his policies, but Congress defeated his plan. Despite the stalemate between the progressive Roosevelt and a reluctant Congress, Roosevelt ran for a third term. Roosevelt believed that Adolf Hitler intended to conquer Europe, which would be helpless to resist without support from the United States. Although Americans were reluctant to be involved in another world war, Roosevelt won by a narrow majority. However, the decision to enter the war was made for Roosevelt by the Japanese on December 7, 1941, and the White House became headquarters for those who controlled the strategy of World War II.

Exhausted by the political rigors of war, Roosevelt went to Warm Springs, Georgia, in the spring of 1945, and on the morning of April 12, he suffered a massive cerebral hemorrhage and died.

Alfred Emanuel Smith

Alfred Emanuel Smith was born on December 30, 1873. He left school after his father's death and took a series of odd jobs. At twenty-one, Smith attended his first political meeting and became interested in a local contest, in which he supported a candidate opposed to Tammany Hall, the powerful local executive committee of the Democratic Party. He decided to enter politics and in 1903 was elected to the New York State assembly, representing a tenement district of New York City.

In 1918, Smith was elected to the first of four terms as governor of New York. As a reformer he was influenced by the city's 1911 Triangle Waist Coat fire, a disaster that killed 146 workers, most of them women. Smith launched an investigation of factory conditions, sponsored bills regulating wages and hours of women and children, provided increased workers' compensation, and enforced sanitary, health, and fire standards. Smith also defended civil liberties and attacked Prohibition.

Smith was the first Roman Catholic nominated for president of the United States. With his brown derby hat, cigar, and colorful speech, Smith came to be known as the champion of urban America. "The Sidewalks of New York" was his presidential campaign theme song. Smith encountered bitter opposition from agricultural communities, Protestant leaders, Prohibitionists, and the Ku Klux Klan. Although Smith lost the 1928 election to Herbert Hoover, his candidacy symbolized the aspirations of immigrant groups—he carried the nation's twelve largest cities.

Although Smith supported Roosevelt in 1932, he became a bitter foe of the New Deal. Smith believed that the New Deal compromised the Constitution, eroded states' rights, and threatened individual liberty. Along with others who opposed the New Deal, Smith founded the American Liberty League, supporting Republican candidates for president in 1936 and 1940.

Smith eventually left politics and became president of Empire State, Inc., which erected and operated the Empire State Building in New York City. Smith died in New York City in 1944.

Eugene Talmadge

Eugene Talmadge was born in Forsyth, Georgia, on September 23, 1884. He graduated from the University of Georgia in 1907 and practiced law in Atlanta before moving to Montgomery. Talmadge successfully ran for the office of commissioner of agriculture in 1926 and six years later he was elected governor of Georgia. Talmadge was twice defeated for the Democratic nomination for the U.S. Senate but was reelected Georgia's governor in 1934, 1940, and 1946.

Talmadge supported a form of populism that called for decreased taxes on one hand and increased government programs on the other. His main support came from farmers, and his right-wing views earned him the nickname "Wild Man from Sugar Creek." Talmadge was also an outspoken opponent of President Franklin Roosevelt and his New Deal policies. Talmadge described the Civilian Conservation Corps as "bums and loafers." He also opposed the National Labor Relations Board, and when a textile strike broke out in 1934, Talmadge declared martial law and sent troops to deal with the strikers.

Talmadge also opposed black civil rights and in 1941, attempted to fire two university administrators, allegedly for advocating integrated public schools. When the board of regents refused, Talmadge dismissed all of them and replaced them with people who supported him. As a result, Georgia's public colleges and universities lost their accreditation, which aroused much resentment, and in 1942, he lost the Democratic gubernatorial nomination. Talmadge had strong support among the rural counties, however, and became governor-elect again in 1946, but he died before taking office.

Norman Mattoon Thomas

Norman Mattoon Thomas, the son of a Presbyterian minister, was born in Marion, Ohio, on November 20, 1884. He studied political science under Woodrow Wilson at Princeton University and graduated in 1905. Thomas did voluntary social work in New York before studying theology at the Union Theological Seminary. Following his graduation, Thomas accepted the pastorate of the East Harlem Church and the chairmanship of the American Parish, a settlement house in one of the poorest sections of New York City.

In 1920, Thomas joined with Jane Addams, Elizabeth Gurley Flynn, and Upton Sinclair to establish the American Civil Liberties Union and in 1921 became associate editor of the influential liberal weekly the *Nation*. In 1922, Thomas was made executive codirector of the League for Industrial Democracy, a position he held for more than ten years.

Influenced by the writings of the Christian Socialist movement in Britain, Thomas became a committed socialist, and in 1918, Thomas joined the Socialist Party. He was the party's candidate for governor of New York in 1924, and, after the death of Eugene Debs, the party's presidential candidate in 1928, 1932, and 1936. Although easily defeated, Thomas had the satisfaction of seeing Franklin D. Roosevelt introduce several measures that Thomas had advocated during his presidential campaign. However, Thomas was generally critical of Roosevelt's New Deal administration, holding that it stressed solution of economic emergencies to the neglect of moral issues.

Thomas was a strong critic of Soviet communism, and after the war he lectured and wrote extensively on the need for world disarmament and the easing of cold war tensions. In 1955 he resigned his official posts in the Socialist Party but remained its chief spokesman until shortly before his death. His works include *The Conscientious Objector in America* (1923), *Socialism of Our Time* (1929), *Human Exploitation* (1934), *Appeal to the Nations* (1947), *Socialist's Faith* (1951), *The Test of Freedom* (1954), *The Prerequisite for Peace* (1959), *Great Dissenters* (1961), and *Socialism Reexamined* (1963).

Henry Wallace

Henry Agard Wallace was born in 1886. After graduating from Iowa State College with a bachelor of science degree in agriculture in 1910, he became associate editor of *Wallaces' Farmer*, one of the leading farm journals in the United States, succeeding his father as editor in 1924. Wallace also developed several high-yielding strains of hybrid corn, selling the seed with great success through his own company.

Originally a Republican, Wallace supported the Democratic presidential candidate Alfred E. Smith in 1928, and in 1932 he helped swing Iowa for Franklin D. Roosevelt. As secretary of agriculture during the first two Roosevelt administrations, he was an ardent supporter of New Deal policies, and set up within the Department of Agriculture the Agricultural Adjustment Administration to administer the farm price support program.

In 1940, Wallace was elected vice president and served in this capacity during Roosevelt's third term in office. In 1944, after the nomination of Harry S. Truman as vice president, Wallace was appointed secretary of commerce and confirmed to that position by the Senate on March 1, 1945, shortly before Truman succeeded to the presidency. A speech Wallace made on September 12, 1946, attacking the administration's firm policy toward the Soviet Union, led to his resignation by presidential request. He then became editor of the liberal weekly the *New Republic*, whose circulation more than doubled before he left in 1947.

In 1948, Wallace became presidential candidate of the Progressive Party, a newly organized third party with a pro-Soviet platform attacking the Marshall Plan and calling for disarmament. Although polling a popular vote of over a million, Wallace and the vice presidential candidate, Senator Glen H. Taylor of Idaho, failed to carry any state. Wallace withdrew from politics and resumed his activity with the Pioneer Hi-Bred Corn Company from his farm in New York State.

Wallace was a prolific writer. His publications include *Corn and Corn-Growing* (1923), *America Must Choose* (1934), and *Sixty Million Jobs* (1945).

William Allen White

William Allen White, born in Emporia, Kansas, on February 10, 1868, was an American journalist known as the "Sage of Emporia." His mixture of tolerance, optimism, liberal Republicanism, and provincialism made him the epitome of the small-town American.

White learned the printer's trade on the *El Dorado Republican* under T.P. Fulton and in 1891 joined the staff of the *Kansas City Journal*. White purchased the *Emporia Gazette*, which he edited until his death in 1944. White's editorial "What's the Matter with Kansas," published on August 15, 1896, attacked populism, a doctrine dedicated to agrarian interests. White gained favor with McKinley Republicans and a national reputation when his editorial was distributed by the Republican Party, helping elect William McKinley over Democrat William Jennings Bryan.

Although White was a lifelong Republican, he supported the

Progressive ("Bull Moose") candidacy of Theodore Roosevelt in 1912. In addition, White ran as an independent for governor of Kansas in 1924 because of his opposition to the Ku Klux Klan. In later years, he chaired the internationalist and bipartisan Committee to Defend America by Aiding the Allies, which supported Franklin D. Roosevelt's efforts to make the United States an active supporter of those resisting Hitler in 1940.

In 1922, White found himself facing arrest and a possible jail sentence brought on by a public argument about labor rights and free speech with then–Kansas governor Henry Allen. After charges against him were dropped, White penned his Pulitzer Prize–winning editorial on the freedom of speech, "To an Anxious Friend." It ran in the *Emporia Gazette* on July 27, 1922.

Aubrey Williams

Aubrey Williams, the son of a blacksmith, was born in 1890 in Springville, Alabama, where he observed the problems of racism and poverty. Williams served as a student pastor from 1911 through 1916 at Maryville College in Tennessee. After service in the YMCA, the French Foreign Legion, and the U.S. Army, he turned to a career in social work, graduating from the University of Cincinnati in 1921.

Williams was a staunch advocate of programs for women and children, believing that the government had a role in promoting social justice. A protege of Harry Hopkins, administrative head of the Works Progress Administration (WPA), Williams was selected as the national director of the National Youth Administration (NYA), established on June 26, 1935. The purpose of the NYA was to provide education, jobs, recreation, and counseling for youths between the ages of sixteen and twenty-five. The Student Aid Program paid students for working on campus, helping them stay in school. Williams also sought to promote racial equality. A fund was set aside to help promising African American graduate students. Approximately two hundred African American students received Ph.D.s during the 1930s compared with only forty-five between 1900 and 1930.

Before the New Deal slowed to a halt in 1938, Williams helped ensure that his relief agencies were the most racially enlightened of all the alphabet agencies. He even forced the NYA state director of Alabama to integrate social gatherings of the agency. In 1943, when Williams left the NYA, nearly 5 million of the nation's unschooled youth had filled New Deal jobs he helped create.

Ellen S. Woodward

Ellen S. Woodward (1887–1974) was touted as President Franklin D. Roosevelt's second most powerful woman appointee. Among American women only Eleanor Roosevelt and Labor Department secretary Frances Perkins could claim more elevated roles in the circle of FDR's administration. She was also the first southern woman to hold a top-ranking position in a federal administration.

Woodward, the daughter of a lawyer, was born on July 11, 1887, in Oxford, Mississippi. When her mother died of tuberculosis in 1895, Woodward began to follow her father to work and into the courtroom. She enjoyed her home schooling in politics when her family moved to Washington, D.C., where her father served in both the House and the Senate, recalling, "I grew up in an atmosphere of politics, where government affairs—local, state and national—were constantly discussed."

Woodward married an attorney and raised her family in Louisville, Mississippi, where her work in Mississippi women's clubs focused her civic work. Her reform spirit seemed grounded in a conviction that progress was synonymous with a community's growth and economic well-being. During World War I, she became involved in local defense efforts, becoming chair of the Women's Committee of the Council of National Defense.

In 1925, Woodward completed her husband's term in the Mississippi legislature after he died of a heart attack. She supported Franklin D. Roosevelt in his bid for the presidency and was appointed to a position as director of women's work relief under three successive New Deal agencies from 1933 to 1938. Woodward made extraordinary inroads on behalf of unemployed women. Although Americans had not yet recognized women as part of the workforce, Woodward's efforts to help poor women were considerable in view of American attitudes at that time. Woodward was an administrator for the Works Progress Administration, later serving on the Social Security Board. After the board was abolished in 1946, she served with the Federal Security Agency until her retirement in 1954.

Chronology

1928
March 4: Herbert Hoover is inaugurated as the thirty-first president of the United States.

1929
October 29: The stock market crashes.

November 19–27: Hoover convenes several conferences with the leading spokesmen of industry, finance, agriculture, the Federal Reserve system, and public utilities.

1930
June: Congress passes the Smoot-Hawley Tariff Act to raise agricultural duties, which brings retaliatory tariff acts from foreign countries; U.S. foreign trade suffers a sharp decline, and the depression intensifies.

October: Hoover forms the President's Emergency Committee for Employment (PECE).

December: The once-powerful Bank of the United States, along with many smaller banks, fails.

1931
A severe drought hits the midwestern and southern plains.

November 7: The National Credit Corporation opens for business but fails to encourage investment.

December 11: New York Bank of the United States collapses.

1932
February/March: The Reconstruction Finance Corporation (RFC) approves loans to banks, railroads, and lending institutions, but no industrial recovery follows.

July 21: Hoover signs the Emergency Relief and Construction Act, but funds fall short and delays keep programs from being implemented.

November 8: Franklin Delano Roosevelt defeats Hoover and becomes the thirty-second president of the United States.

1933

March 4: Roosevelt delivers his inaugural address, warning, "The only thing we have to fear is fear itself," and begins what becomes known as the first hundred days of the New Deal.

March 9: Congress passes the Emergency Banking Relief Act, which provides for the reopening of banks as soon as examiners find them to be financially secure.

March 31: The Reforestation Relief Act creates the Civilian Conservation Corps (CCC) with 250,000 immediate jobs for men ages eighteen to twenty-five.

April 19: The United States goes off the gold standard.

May 12: Congress establishes the Federal Emergency Relief Administration (FERA) and allocates an initial fund of $500 million to help those in need; the Agricultural Adjustment Act (AAA) pays farmers not to grow crops; the Emergency Farm Mortgage Act allots $200 million for refinancing to help farmers facing foreclosure.

May 18: Congress creates the Tennessee Valley Authority.

May 27: Congress passes the Federal Securities Act, which requires the government to register and approve all issues of stocks and bonds.

June 16: The second Banking Act of 1933, Glass-Steagall, gives the Federal Reserve Board tighter control of the investment practices of banks and creates the Federal Deposit Insurance Corporation (FDIC); Congress establishes the National Industrial Recovery Act (NIRA), which creates the National Recovery Administration, and in turn, the Public Works Administration (PWA); Congress gives the PWA permission to spend $3.3 billion for various public works projects.

November 8: Roosevelt creates the Civil Works Administration (CWA) to build roads, parks, airports, and other facilities, giving jobs to 4 million unemployed Americans.

1934

Spring/Summer: More than a million and a half American workers go on strike.

June: Congress passes the Frazier-Lemke Farm Bankruptcy Act, restricting the ability of banks to dispossess farmers in times of distress.

June 6: The Securities Exchange Act of 1934 delegates responsibility for enforcement to the Securities and Exchange Commission (SEC).

June 19: The Communications Act of 1934 creates the Federal Communications Commission (FCC).

Summer: Hundreds of thousands of residents of the dust bowl states, including Oklahoma, Arkansas, and Texas, migrate to nearby states.

1935

Winter: The Supreme Court declares the NIRA unconstitutional.

February 26: Congress passes the Soil Conservation Act to support farm income by making soil-conservation and soil-building payments to participating farmers.

April 8: Roosevelt approves the Emergency Relief Appropriation Act, which provides $525 million for drought relief.

May 6: Roosevelt creates the Works Progress Administration (WPA).

July 5: Congress establishes the National Labor Relations Act, also known as the Wagner Act, to help protect trade unionists from their employers; now protected from their employer retribution, union membership grows rapidly.

August 14: Congress passes the Social Security Act, which establishes old-age pensions, unemployment insurance, and welfare.

1936

February 17: The Supreme Court upholds the constitutionality of the Tennessee Valley Authority.

May 11: Congress passes the Rural Electrification Act to construct and operate electric systems and generating plants.

November 3: Roosevelt is reelected president, defeating Alfred M. Landon.

1937
February 5: Roosevelt submits a proposal asking Congress to expand the number of Supreme Court justices. Congress defeats the plan in July.

April 12: The Supreme Court declares constitutional provisions of the NLRA of 1935 that guarantee workers the right to unionize.

May: Economic recovery stops, and the economy enters a second depression.

July: Congress passes the Bankhead-Jones Farm Tenancy Act to provide federal loans to farm tenants to purchase land.

September 1: Congress passes the National Housing (Wagner-Steagall) Act, creating the U.S. Housing Authority (USHA).

1938
February 16: Congress passes a second Agricultural Adjustment Act.

June: Economic recovery begins; Congress passes the Fair Labor Standards Act, which establishes a national minimum wage and limits work hours, and the Food, Drug, and Cosmetic Act, which requires scientific proof that new products can be safely used before putting them on the market.

1939
Fall: Rain finally brings an end to drought.

September 3: Germany invades Poland. England and France declare war on Germany, and World War II begins in Europe.

1940
June 13: Roosevelt signs a $1.3 billion defense bill.

November 5: Roosevelt is again reelected president, defeating Wendell Wilkie.

December 7: Japanese planes bomb Pearl Harbor, Hawaii, and the United States enters World War II.

For Further Research

Oratorical Collections

JAMES ANDREWS AND DAVID ZAREFSKY, EDS., *American Voices: Significant Speeches in American History 1640–1945*. White Plains, NY: Longman, 1989.

ALBERT CRAIG BAIRD, ED., *American Public Addresses, 1740–1952*. New York: McGraw-Hill, 1956.

JOHN GRAHAM, ED., *Great American Speeches, 1898–1963*. New York: Appleton-Century-Crofts, 1970.

HERBERT HOOVER, *Addresses upon the American Road, 1933–1938*. New York: Scribners, 1938.

CHARLES HURD, *A Treasury of Great American Speeches: Our Country's Life and History in the Words of Its Great Men*. New York: Hawthorn, 1959.

General Studies

FREDERICK LEWIS ALLEN, *Since Yesterday: The Nineteen-Thirties in America, September 3, 1929–September 3, 1939*. New York: Harper & Brothers, 1940.

JOHN F. BAUMAN AND THOMAS H. COODE, *In the Eye of the Great Depression: New Deal Reporters and the Agony of the American People*. DeKalb: Northern Illinois University Press, 1988.

MATHEW PAUL BONNIFIELD, *The Dust Bowl: Men, Dirt, and Depression*. Albuquerque: University of New Mexico Press, 1979.

GLEN H. ELDER JR., *Children of the Great Depression*. Boulder, CO: Westview, 1998.

EDWARD R. ELLIS, *A Nation in Torment: The Great Depression, 1929–1939*. New York: Capricorn, 1970.

ROBERT MCELVAINE, *The Great Depression: America 1929–1941*. New York: Times, 1984.

MICHAEL E. PARRISH, *Anxious Decades: America in Prosperity and Depression, 1920–1941*. New York: W.W. Norton, 1992.

STUDS TERKEL, *Hard Times: An Oral History of the Great Depression*. New York: Random House, 1970.

T.H. WATKINS, *The Great Depression: America in the 1930s*. Boston: Little, Brown, 1993.

The New Deal

ANTHONY J. BADGER, *The New Deal: The Depression Years, 1933–1940*. New York: Farrar, Straus and Giroux, 1989.

ALAN BRINKLEY, *Voices of Protest: Huey Long, Father Coughlin, and the Great Depression*. New York: Random House, 1983.

BRUCE I. BUSTARD, *A New Deal for the Arts*. Seattle: University of Washington Press, 1997.

ROBERT EDEN, *The New Deal and Its Legacy*. Westport, CT: Greenwood, 1989.

RONALD EDSFORTH, *The New Deal: America's Response to the Great Depression*. Malden, MA: Blackwell, 2000.

LESLIE ALEXANDER LACY, *The Soil Soldiers: The Civilian Conservation Corps in the Great Depression*. Radnor, PA: Chilton, 1976.

ARTHUR M. SCHLESINGER JR., *The Coming of the New Deal*. Boston: Houghton Mifflin, 1959.

SUSAN WARE, *Beyond Suffrage: Women in the New Deal*. Boston: Harvard University Press, 1981.

HOWARD ZINN, ED., *New Deal Thought*. Indianapolis: Bobbs-Merrill, 1966.

Social and Cultural Impact of the Depression

TERRY A. COONEY, *Balancing Acts: American Thought and Culture in the 1930s*. New York: Twayne, 1995.

JOHN B. KIRBY, *Black Americans in the Roosevelt Era: Liberalism and Race*. Knoxville: University of Tennessee Press, 1980.

ERNEST W. MAY, "Charity During the Great Depression," *American Enterprise*, May 1996.

JANET MONTEFIORE, *Men and Women Writers of the 1930s: The Dangerous Flood of History*. New York: Routledge, 1996.

ERROL LINCOLN UYS, *Riding the Rails: Teenagers on the Move During the Great Depression*. New York: Penguin, 1993.

SUSAN WARE, *Holding Their Own: American Women in the 1930s*. Boston: Twayne, 1982.

Biographical Studies

KENNETH S. DAVIS, *FDR: The New Deal Years 1933–1937*. New York: Random House, 1986.

HERBERT HOOVER, *The Memoirs of Herbert Hoover: 1929–1941: The Great Depression*. New York: Macmillan, 1952.

HAROLD L. ICKES, *The Secret Diary of Harold L. Ickes: The First Thousand Days, 1933–1936*. New York: Simon & Schuster, 1954.

WILLIAM LEUCHTENBURG, *Franklin D. Roosevelt and the New Deal, 1932–1940*. New York: Harper and Row, 1963.

FRANCES PERKINS, *The Roosevelt I Knew*. New York: Harper and Row, 1946.

ELEANOR ROOSEVELT, *This I Remember*. New York: Harper and Brothers, 1949.

GENE SMITH, *The Shattered Dream: Herbert Hoover and the Great Depression*. New York: Morrow, 1970.

Websites

A&E TELEVISION NETWORKS, *The History Channel—Speeches*, www.historychannel.com/speeches.

FRANKLIN AND ELEANOR ROOSEVELT INSTITUTE, *The New Deal Network: A Guide to the Great Depression of the 1930s*, http://newdeal.feri.org.

PUBLIC BROADCASTING SYSTEM, *Great American Speeches*, www.pbs.org/greatspeeches.

Index

vs. direct relief, 83–84
is not socialist, 183
philosophy behind, 81–82, 84–85
projects of, 85–86
satisfaction from, 82–83
and solving unemployment problem,
89–90
for women, 86–89
Works Relief Act, 196
work-study jobs, 22
see also National Youth
Administration

World War II, 21

youth
desires of, 110
educational problems facing,
100–101
enrolled in higher education, 108
faith in, 110–11
New Deal funding for, 21–22
see also National Youth
Administration